UNLOCKING
POTENTIAL

———

Unlocking Potential

How Great Leaders Get the Most Out of
Individuals, Teams & Organizations
Copyright 2021 by Ben Bergeron

Write Hand Media
All rights reserved.

ISBN:
Paperback: 9798759763246
Hardcover: 9798759794349

FROM THE BESTSELLING AUTHORS OF
CHASING EXCELLENCE

UNLOCKING POTENTIAL

HOW GREAT LEADERS GET THE
MOST OUT OF INDIVIDUALS,
TEAMS & ORGANIZATIONS

BEN BERGERON

with Christine Bald

For Nick Jeffries
The best teammate in the game

CONTENTS

"

TRIAL
BY FIRE.

CrossFit New England, traditional

———

TRIAL BY FIRE

What is the opposite of Christmas Eve? That's what I'm feeling as I drive to CrossFit New England (CFNE) on my
first day of work. Given the ungodly hour—4:45 a.m.—you might
assume my dominant emotion would be sleepiness. Or disbelief,
which is how I felt when Ben Bergeron emailed me my coaching
schedule last week. Five thirty and six thirty? In the *morning*? *Every* weekday? *Yo.* In the moment, however, any lingering tiredness
or shock are being overridden by a much stronger emotion: abject
terror. I am about to coach my very first class at one of the best
CrossFit gyms in the world, a task for which I feel comically unpre-
pared. I have been coaching for years, but every gym is different.
How are classes supposed to flow at CFNE? How do they usually
warm up? How do they set up equipment? When is the bathroom
break? The one CFNE class I attended—three days ago—did not

provide nearly enough data to answer these questions. I feel like I'm about to take a midterm exam after skipping every lecture all semester.

By the time I get to the gym, I am so nervous I can barely think. I have that terrible pre-competition feeling that is a hybrid of nerves and nausea. This is exacerbated when I walk in and note that there are, oddly, already a lot of people here. It's pitch black outside but shit is positively lit inside CFNE. There are so many people, in fact, that for a brief moment I'm terrified that I misread my schedule. *Does class start at 5:00 a.m? Am I late on my first day?* No, no, it's okay. But what are all these people doing here already? In an effort to find out, I make small talk with some of the members before class starts. Everyone seems to be named Mike; at least, I can't remember any other names besides Mike. I am smiling on the outside but basically dying on the inside. All my organs are doing backflips. My heart is beating so loudly I'm surprised no one else can hear it.

At exactly 5:30 a.m., Head Coach Harry Palley looks at me and asks if I'm ready. "Absolutely," I lie. He cups his hands to his mouth and bellows, "Five thirty, bring it in!" It's not until this moment that I realize how many people are actually here. As the group circles up, my sense of dread deepens. There must be close to fifty athletes in this class. If Harry finds this unusual, he doesn't show it. To me, it's not unusual. It's lunacy. I've never coached a class larger than eighteen people. Everyone is looking at me as if they are keenly aware of this fact. Can I do this? I don't have a choice. It's happening. I take a deep breath and start class.

A loud, confident voice that I recognize as my own instructs the class to grab barbells and make two lines. I begin the warmup with burpees, which elicits immediate outcry. You would have thought I asked them to warm up with muscle-ups. Warming up with exercise at a fitness class? It is an outrage. One of the Mikes looks like he wants to call the police. In less than twenty seconds, I have managed to make everyone in this room despise me. Everything about this feels foreign. Up until this moment, I have never been a new coach. Even when I started at CrossFit Hierarchy, the Washington, D.C., gym I helped run for three years, I knew every member by name and had a relationship with them. By the time I left, I was loved and trusted. Standing in front of this group, miles away from either, I'm hit with a daunting thought: *I am starting over completely.* I have no credibility with these people. It's going to take weeks for them to like me and months for them to trust me. This is not just going to be hard and uncomfortable today. It's going to be hard and uncomfortable for a long time. I file that thought away for later and begin coaching.

The workout is two parts: a heavy three-rep front squat followed by a metcon (CrossFit parlance for "cardio") of rowing, deadlifts and box jumps. It's been named "Natick Hammer," presumably because it's been designed to smash my will to live. The squatting is straightforward enough, but there are not nearly enough rowers, bumper plates or plyo boxes for this enormous class. This is not lost on Harry, who has been observing my class from afar like a lifeguard. I must look like I'm drowning because he walks over and throws me a life raft. "What do you think about changing the workout?" he asks. "Errrrr," I reply knowledgeably. *My dude, it took me two hours to write the lesson plan I have. I'm not emotionally prepared to freestyle on my first day.*

Harry starts explaining how we can adapt the workout to teams of three. He's saying words, but I'm so rattled that I can't process any of them. I just stand there looking confused. At length, he realizes I'm mentally handicapped and mercifully steps in to brief the class on how we're going to change the workout. Just when I've wrapped my head around the new format, Harry comes back. "Actually, I don't think that's going to work either," he admits. "I think we gotta do it as an EMOM instead." This is like being awake during your own surgery. I have no clue what he's talking about, and I'm painfully conscious of how incompetent I must seem. By the time the class returns from the pre-WOD bathroom break, Harry has fully taken command of the class. I feel like a failure. I'm a better coach than this, but I'm not being allowed to show it. This was not how today was supposed to go. There were not supposed to be fifty people here. CrossFit New England isn't supposed to run out of equipment. I wonder briefly if anyone has ever been fired after one class.

●

Everything about my first day was the result of poor leadership. Leadership is about helping people succeed, and my first day at CFNE was pretty much the opposite of that. I couldn't be the coach I knew I was that day (or many days after that) because I experienced every class as a series of intense firefights, completely and utterly distracted by fear. The lack of any kind of onboarding process meant I had no idea what was expected of me or how to succeed. I had to figure it out on my own, using roughly the same method Thomas Edison used to discover the lightbulb—by exhausting all the wrong ways first. For a brand-new employee desperately trying to make a good impression, this was fairly traumatizing. For the next month, starting around 8 p.m. the night before I coached, I had extreme anxiety about the next day's class. This anxiety prevented me from being myself in front of the room, which is why it took three months or so for the members to fully warm up to me.

If a story about poor leadership strikes you as an unconventional way to introduce a book about leadership, you're not alone. Ben had the same thought. So I'll tell you what I told him: The brilliance of Ben's leadership is that he is not a "natural leader," whatever that means. For one thing, he's a shy introvert—ten times out of ten, Ben would rather be at home than at any social gathering. He's also not what anyone would consider a "people person." As good as he is in front of a room, small talk makes him want to low-key die. When faced with problems within his organization, Ben's first instinct is to solve them himself; it takes a great deal of discipline for him to delegate things to his team. The point is, Ben lacks many of the qualities typically associated with great leaders. The enormous success he's had as a CrossFit Games coach and business owner camouflages the fact that his leadership hasn't always been great, or even very good. To become who he is today, Ben had to override a lot of his factory settings. That, in essence, is what this book is about. It is the story of Ben's evolution as a leader.

That is why I'm writing the foreword of this book, despite the fact that—unless you happened to notice my name on the cover—you have never heard of me: I've been around for a whole lot of it. In my various capacities working for Ben over the last six years—CFNE coach, CompTrain media director, *Chasing Excellence* ghostwriter—I have had a front-row seat to the evolution of his leadership and experienced it firsthand. The story I told you about my first day, for example, would never happen at CFNE now—Ben's entire leadership philosophy is about creating an environment in which people and teams can be completely focused on the task at hand and perform to their full potential.

I can personally attest that he's great at it. In this book, Ben and I define a leader as someone who helps others achieve more than they could on their own. There is no better description of Ben's impact on my life. So many of my proudest moments over the last six years—passing my CrossFit Level 3 exam, putting CompTrain on the map, writing *Chasing Excellence*—are things I would not have accomplished without him. After that first day at CFNE, Ben became my own personal Mr. Miyagi, carving out twenty minutes after every single six thirty a.m. class I coached to give me feedback and help me improve. His mentoring was so effective that when he pushed me to take the notoriously difficult CrossFit Level 3 exam a year later, I passed without studying at all. A few months after that, Ben convinced me I could write a book when I doubted my qualifications to step up as his ghostwriter. "All you have to do is write the next chapter," he said. "Don't think about it as a whole book. It's one chapter at a time. We'll write this chapter. Then we'll write the next one." I took his advice, and the book I very much did not want to write became an Amazon bestseller and launched my career as a professional writer.

Even my accomplishments that have apparently nothing to do with Ben have everything to do with Ben. The culture of CFNE, which he painstakingly and intentionally cultivates, has taught me so much more than just how to see and correct functional movement. One of the values that underpins CFNE culture is "hungry," which we define in several different ways. One of them is "Be proactive," something Ben has (as you'll see in this book) brought to life in dozens of different ways over the years. Which explains why, when it occurred to me that someone should tell the amazing and unlikely story of the 2020 CrossFit Games season, I didn't shrug and wait to see who would do it. I wrote Dave Castro a letter and mailed it to him with examples of exactly the kind of story I wanted to write. When Dave invited me to the Games in Aromas, California, to do just that, I silently thanked Ben. Without him and the culture he built at CFNE, I wouldn't have landed that job—because it wouldn't even have occurred to me to ask for it. Before I moved to Boston, I would have regarded the idea of telling the director of the CrossFit Games how to tell the story of his own event as wildly presumptuous to the point of arrogance. The years I spent immersed in CFNE's culture remade me on a molecular level. Thanks to Ben, I am no longer the kind of person who waits for things to fall into my lap. The proactive character trait that friends and strangers often applaud me for is not one I was born with—it's a product of the culture at CrossFit New England, handmade by Ben Bergeron.

It's easy for me to see how Ben's leadership has helped me achieve more than I ever could have on my own. It has taken me much longer to appreciate how his leadership has made me a better *person* than I would have become on my own. If you read *Chasing*

Excellence, you know that Ben looks for certain character traits in his athletes: integrity, honesty, humility and growth-mindedness, to name a few of the big ones. When it comes to his staff, Ben takes it a step further. He has to. Like every CrossFit affiliate owner, his goal is to help his members change their lives. Changing lives, of course, is not easy work. Inspiring that kind of change starts with inspiring trust, which starts with relationships; that is, the ability to connect with people and make them feel important and understood. At CFNE, we call this "people smart." Most people call it "emotional intelligence." Either way, it's an essential skill for any CrossFit coach, and Ben developed mine with the same vigor he developed my traditional coaching skills. I am here to tell you that the former is much, *much* more uncomfortable than the latter. As you might imagine, it's not fun to have someone constantly pointing out your character flaws. "Christine, your colleagues don't enjoy working with you sometimes," for example, hits different than, "Christine, your teaching progressions for the snatch needs work." It often felt like I was being tried at The Hague. On more than one occasion, I've wished that Ben would be *less* committed to my personal growth—I don't know how many times he's made me cry over the years, but it's a lot. It occurs to me now that as painful as that growth was for me, it was probably just as painful for him. Ben is a deeply sensitive person who wants to be loved by the people he leads; giving tough personal feedback goes against his very nature. That he chose to do it anyway is more than an act of great leadership. It's an act of extraordinary friendship. No matter how hard those conversations were for us, Ben never stopped having them with me. He never stopped challenging me to grow my emotional intelligence, even when I repeatedly missed the mark.

When I look back on the person I was when I moved to Boston, I feel nothing but profound gratitude. I am a much, much better person because of Ben's leadership. It is not an exaggeration to say that every single relationship I have with every single person in my life is richer and deeper because of Ben.

Ben's leadership style may not be for everyone (I see you, Reddit). But you can't deny it works. Two successful businesses. Multiple CrossFit Games champions. A bestselling book (hopefully two, amiright). A popular podcast. A loving family. Before we get into the leadership principles that have enabled all that success, it's worth reflecting on this point a little longer: **Before he was a great leader, Ben was a pretty bad leader.** The thing that makes him a great leader is not some inborn aptitude for leadership. It is that he is fully committed to becoming a great leader and never stops trying to get better at it. It's impossible to read this book without appreciating something I've witnessed up close for years: Ben is who he is because works at it—*hard.*

As someone with a similarly low natural aptitude for leadership, I am encouraged by this. We all should be. Ben is living proof that leadership is not some inherent trait we're either born with or not. Leadership is a skill and, like any skill, it can be learned and improved—if you're willing to really work at it. If you are, Ben Bergeron is one of the best coaches you could hope for.

And I would know.

— CHRISTINE BALD, Co-Author

Chasing Excellence & *Unlocking Potential*

"

IT IS THE LONG HISTORY
OF HUMANKIND (AND
ANIMAL KIND, TOO) THAT
THOSE WHO LEARNED
TO COLLABORATE
AND IMPROVISE MOST
EFFECTIVELY HAVE
PREVAILED.

———

Charles Darwin

FLOW

I n 2019, a record eighty thousand spectators attended the Cross-Fit Games to watch the fittest men and women in the world vie for the title of Fittest On Earth. One year later that number is ... zero. The fact that the Games are happening at all in 2020 feels like a miracle. CrossFit, the sport's organizing body, has—like the organizing bodies of sports everywhere—had to get creative to pull it off amid a global pandemic that is, by the third week of October, still raging. The result is a CrossFit Games unlike any in the history of the sport. For one thing, it features the smallest field of competitors ever—just five male and five female athletes were invited to contend in the "finals" (down from three hundred last year). The most striking change, however, is the scenery. The CrossFit Games have been uprooted from their usual Midwestern venue and temporarily returned to their ancestral home in Aromas, California.

It is the end of the first day of competition and one of the athletes I coach, Katrin Davíðsdóttir, steps onto a dusty red starting mat for the start of Event 4, a trail run of undisclosed distance named "Ranch Loop." The Ranch is the most famous address in CrossFit—it's where the Games were held for the first time in 2007. Prior to the 2020 season, the sport had long since outgrown the Ranch; the Games upgraded to a larger venue in 2010, then again to a still larger complex in 2017. Very few CrossFit Games athletes have had the privilege of competing here in Aromas, but Katrin is one of them—she was among the forty women who were flown here from Carson, California, during the 2016 Games, which began with another trail run of undisclosed distance. Then, as now, I'm watching Katrin compete from afar; while coaches are allowed in the CrossFit Games bubble, they are not permitted to accompany their athletes to The Ranch. I don't mind—the strict COVID-19 safety precautions are the only reason any of us get to be here at all. Still, it's why I'm watching the trail run event the same way everyone else is: via the livestream on CrossFit's YouTube channel.

For the first thirty minutes, Ranch Loop is indistinguishable from the course used in 2016—lots of dust, lots of hills, lots of trees. But then the first athletes round the final turn, and the event changes completely. After running 5k, the leaders cross what we all assume is the finish line. They are immediately beckoned by CrossFit Games Director Dave Castro, who gestures and points animatedly. After a moment of confusion, the pair of male leaders—Mat Fraser and Justin Medeiros—do a one-eighty and trot off in the direction from which they just came. It dawns on us at the same time it dawns on them: *This isn't the finish line. It's the halfway point.*

When Katrin reaches the turnaround and receives the news, she is in second to last place. But then something odd happens. Katrin starts catching up. Half a kilometer after the halfway point, she overtakes one of her competitors. Half a klick after that, she picks off another. After two kilometers, she's out in front. She extends her lead during the remainder of the race and crosses the finish line first by a significant margin.

After the event, a sideline reporter asks Katrin how she did it. How was she able to make up so much ground in the second half of such an exhausting race? In her answer, Kat describes the feeling at the halfway point as a kind of focusing moment, in which the outside world faded away. "I love twists like that," she says and shrugs, seemingly unsure of how to explain it herself. During the second half of the event, she says, she wasn't thinking about her competitors at all. Her inner critic was quiet, replaced by a feeling of deep contentment as she focused completely on whatever hill she happened to be climbing. Kat says she completely lost track of time—the second half of the event might have taken five minutes or five hours. The hills and other natural obstacles were not exactly effortless, but enthralling. Listening to her describe them, you could be forgiven for thinking she's talking about putting together a jigsaw puzzle and not competing at one of the most grueling competitions in sports. You get the distinct impression that Katrin genuinely enjoyed herself.

What Kat was experiencing during the second half of Ranch Loop is known as a flow state: a kind of heightened consciousness that exists at the intersection of passion, skill and focus. Athletes often describe this feeling as being "in the zone," as Indiana Pacer forward Paul George did after scoring 21 points in the fourth quarter of an NBA playoff game: "I was just in the zone. Regardless of who was guarding me, I felt like that ball was going to go in that net, and that's an incredible feeling." The flow state is similarly incredible to witness: It's New York Yankee pitcher Don Larsen throwing a perfect Game 5 during the 1956 World Series. It's Michael Jordan dropping 63 points against the 1986 Boston Celtics, one of the greatest teams in NBA history. It's Serena Williams clawing her way back from 1-5 in the third set of the Australian Open semifinal to win the match (and eventually the title) in 2003. It's Tiger Woods on any given Sunday at Augusta.

Flow, of course, isn't reserved for athletes—anyone can operate in a flow state. People from a wide range of professions have described the same feeling of competence and control, loss of self-consciousness, and total absorption in the task at hand. Writers often talk about the magic of working in a flow state, where the world melts away and ideas practically spill out of their brain onto the page. Artists who operate in flow states tend to achieve extraordinary things.

In the yoga world, this feeling is known as "mindfulness" and it informs the essence of the practice: a moment-by-moment awareness of one's thoughts, emotions, bodily sensations and surroundings with openness, non-judgment and curiosity. **The key to getting into this state, as the experiences of athletes, musicians and yogis suggest, is the ability to be completely and totally absorbed in the present moment.** As psychologists put it: "In the flow-like state, we exercise control over the contents of our consciousness rather than allowing ourselves to be passively determined by external forces."[1] This explains why the flow state is so elusive—most of us are very infrequently absorbed in the present because we are *distracted*. These distractions are the "external forces" the definition of flow describes. **Distractions are both the inverse of flow and its greatest enemy.**

When we think of "distractions," we tend to think in terms of interruptions—a car alarm going off when you're trying to study for an exam, for example. That is certainly one kind of distrac-

---

1 Csikszentmihalyi, Mihaly. Flow: The Psychology of Optimal Experience. 1st edition, Harper Perennial Modern Classics, 2008.

tion, but distractions exist on a spectrum. The car alarm is on one end, along with all the other distractions we can see, hear, touch and taste. On the other end are *psychological* distractions. They are things like fear, anxiety, doubt, guilt and nervousness. These are the kind of distractions most leaders don't account for. It's not hard to understand why—unlike car alarms and text notifications, we can't see or hear emotions. But they are just as damaging to flow because the effect is the same: they pull our attention away from the present where flow occurs. Imagine, for example, that you're in front of a camera recording a talk that will be watched by hundreds of your peers. If you are nervous about what people will think of your talk while you're delivering it, it is almost impossible to be yourself and deliver the most compelling presentation. The worry clouds your brain, making it difficult for your true self to flow out. You might stumble over your words, lose your train of thought or completely forget parts of what you prepared. Your anxiety about the future, in other words, contaminates the present. This is problematic because the present is the only place where we have any kind of influence—being completely focused in the present is the only way to unlock our full potential. **The trick to getting into a flow state, therefore, is to somehow disable all the distractions that prevent us from focusing.** This includes both the obvious physiological distractions *and* the less obvious psychological ones we can't see. Overriding our subconscious brain is not an easy task, which is why flow is so difficult to access and why we all live in a suboptimal state of underperformance. The only time we come anywhere close to meeting our full potential is in a flow state, when we remove everything blocking our abilities and our ability can flow out.

When people do manage to "get in the zone," they usually regard it as a happy accident—something that occured by chance or luck or divine intervention. Most of the time, this is true. But it doesn't have to be. **Flow can be accessed with intent and purpose.** As a coach, this has become the core of my methodology. Everything I do with my athletes is designed to facilitate a flow state and allow them to spend as much time there as possible. Since the key to flow is being completely present, my job as a coach is to eliminate every conceivable distraction; to create an environment that allows them to focus singularly on the task at hand so that they might achieve the kind of flow that Katrin tapped into during Ranch Loop.

Much less is known about how the flow state applies to groups of people, but the effects are just as potent. Surgeons, for example, will sometimes describe challenging operations as a 'ballet' in which the entire operating team works as a single organism. Most of us are probably most familiar with group flow in sports—those magical games in which everyone on the team seems to click and just sort of *flow* through the plays, as if they share some kind of hive mind. When this occurs, teams perform to the best of their ability.

The most famous example is the United States hockey team's upset victory over the Soviet Union during the 1980 Olympics, known to posterity as "The Miracle on Ice." "Miracle" is the only apparent explanation for how a young team of American amateurs defeated what is universally regarded as the best hockey team ever assembled. It makes for a great story, but the truth is that Team USA didn't win because of a random miracle. They won with flow. The American coach, Herb Brooks, had a special talent for helping his teams tap into it. If you listen to team captain Mike Eruzione describe Brooks's coaching style, you can see the contours of how he went about it: "He wanted players who were willing to get along. He looked at our mental makeup to determine who would fit into the team chemistry." **This is the essence of leadership: creating an environment free from distractions in which our people can get "in the zone" together.**

For organizations who harness it, flow is nothing short of a superpower. It is the most powerful performance enhancer in the world, the number-one independent variable most commonly associated with extraordinary achievement. And while no one can control exactly when they—much less anyone else—enter a flow state, there's quite a bit we can do as leaders to create the optimal environment to allow our teams to tap into flow more often.

That's what this book is about—it takes what I've learned about getting individuals into a flow state and applies it to groups. Over the years, I have—through trial and an astonishing amount of error—learned that the key to unlocking potential is something I call "samepageness." Group flow occurs when everyone is on the same page about who we are, where we're going and how we're going to get there. This is our task as leaders, and it can be broken down into three categories: culture, vision and execution. Together, they represent the three pillars of leadership:

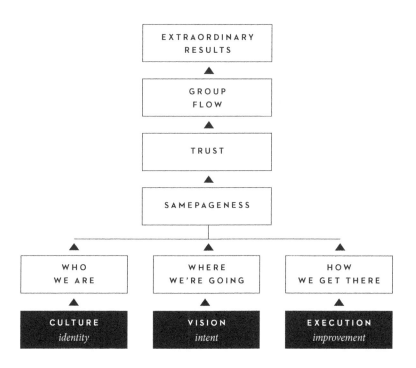

I wish I had this knowledge fifteen years ago. That's why I wrote this book—not because I have attained some wisdom I feel qualified to preach, but because it's the book I wish existed when I was first starting out as a business owner: a guide for building the three pillars of leadership. That's what this book is about. It is a story about unlocking extraordinary group performance, told through the evolution of my two businesses: CrossFit New England and CompTrain. But this book is not just for business owners and CrossFit coaches. It's for anyone who wants to find out just how good their people, teams and organizations can become. This is a leadership book, and we all—at some point in our lives—find ourselves in positions of leadership. Whether you're a parent raising two kids or a vice president managing 150 employees, this book will help you harness the power of group flow in your organization and unlock the full potential of those you lead.

That said, if you put this book down right now and never look at it again, nothing bad will happen. Plenty of organizations—the vast, vast majority, in fact—don't take the time to do any of the things described in these pages, and they're doing just fine. But I'm willing to bet that "fine" isn't your thing. Like me, you're privately horrified by the notion of "good enough." You want to wring every drop of potential out of your people, your team and your organization. For that, transformational leadership is not optional—it's essential. It requires your people to operate in a constant flow state.

Everyone on the team has to be Tom Brady on Super Bowl Sunday—if not every single day, as close to it as possible. That's not the kind of thing that happens organically or by accident. While individuals might be able to occasionally access flow by accident, it is impossible for teams to inadvertently achieve flow. That is because teams have to account for an additional element that individuals do not: social dynamics. Teams are constantly interacting—with each other, with the organization and with the leader. To facilitate flow, these interactions have to meet a very specific set of criteria. Psychologists have identified ten preconditions for group flow that, when met, act as "triggers" that lead to more flow:[2]

---

2   Kotler, Steven. The Rise of Superman: Decoding the Science of Ultimate Human Performance. 1st edition, New Harvest, 2014.

01 FAMILIARITY
People know one another and understand their tics and tendencies

02 BLENDING EGOS
Each person can submerge their ego needs into the group's

03 A SENSE OF CONTROL
Each member of the group feels in control, but still flexible

04 SHARED GOALS
Everyone in the group is working towards the same end

05 CONSTANT COMMUNICATION
A group version of immediate feedback

06 EQUAL PARTICIPATION
Everyone is involved and has roughly similar skill levels

07 SHARED, GROUP RISK
Everyone has some skin in the game

08 YES, AND
Conversations are additive, not combative

09 CLOSE LISTENING
You're paying complete attention to what is being said

10 COMPLETE CONCENTRATION
Total focus in the right here, right now

If you want to understand how to access flow, you have to start by understanding these triggers. As leaders, we have to be able to check off all ten of them within our organizations. I get it; it's daunting. It's a big list. Every item on it is complicated and difficult to pull off. How are we supposed to do ten different things at once, on top of all the day-to-day things we're already doing? It will never be easy, but it doesn't have to be as hard as it seems. Though ostensibly different, **all ten group flow triggers have the same common denominator: Trust. The prerequisite to group flow is *trust.***

So that's where we have to start.

66

I'VE LEARNED THAT PEOPLE WILL FORGET WHAT YOU SAID, PEOPLE WILL FORGET WHAT YOU DID, BUT PEOPLE WILL NEVER FORGET HOW YOU MADE THEM FEEL.

Maya Angelou

01

TRUST

"Oh *God, another sermon about trust."*

I know what you're thinking. In the past, this is where I would have rolled my eyes and put the book down. Trust sounds soft. Intangible. Abstract. And it is all those things, which is why most everyone tends to undervalue it and the role it plays in peak performance. Part of the problem is that we tend to think about trust too narrowly, as either truth or lies. In our minds, people are either honest or they're not. In fact, trust is nowhere near that binary. It's a kaleidoscope of many shades of grey, each of which informs our *belief* in people. When we completely trust someone, we believe that they prioritize our interests equal to or above their own and will always act accordingly. That's what distinguishes the best coaches—their players believe that their coach prioritizes the athlete's success and the team's success over their own personal success. It's the same hallmark of every happy marriage: both partners *believe* that the other person regards their well-being and happiness as more important than their own. This kind of trust is a wonderful feeling, but that's part of the problem. Trust is a feeling, not a rational experience, which might explain why leaders don't take trust seriously. The idea of leading an organization with trust feels akin to treating cancer with holistic "natural" medicine—an approach suitable for hippies and shamans, perhaps, but not for serious people living in the real world. The real world is about logic and reason, not feelings and emotions. That is what informs our approach to leadership.

This attitude, however, is fundamentally wrong. It runs completely counter to human nature. The great irony is that leading with trust is the *ultimate* commitment to logic and reason. Understanding why will make us better leaders. It will allow us to stop viewing trust as a warm and fuzzy soft skill and start appreciating it for what it really is: a cold, hard physiological fact.

THE SCIENCE OF TRUST

Evolutionary psychology exists at the complicated intersection of genetics, neuropsychology, paleobiology and a half-dozen other other sciences, but the central tenet is simple enough to understand: Although human beings today inhabit a thoroughly modern world of self-driving cars, artificial intelligence and space exploration, we do so with the ingrained mentality of Stone Age hunter-gatherers. The primary feature of this ingrained mentality is the primacy of the subconscious part of the brain over every other part of the brain. It is a gift from our ancestors, who, for most of evolutionary history, were not the predators but the prey. Early humans evolved many traits to help them survive, the most powerful of which was a highly sensitive emotional radar—call it instinct. Our ancestors, at the mercy of wild predators and natural disasters, came to rely on these instincts above all else. When they saw or heard a sign of danger—a movement in the grass, a strange shadow—their bodies responded, automatically and almost instantaneously, with a hormonal reaction that acted like a siren warning them of a potential threat. Those who possessed the keenest instincts survived, reproduced and evolved. And, after three hundred thousand years of evolutionary fine-tuning, those instincts are now a permanent feature hardwired into our physiology. **Whether you lead a large company, a medium-sized sports team or a small household, it is essential to understand that human beings have a highly evolved ability to detect danger, and it never turns off.**

What does any of this have to do with getting teams of people into a group flow state? Well, as you'll recall from the introduction, flow is about complete focus in the present moment. But thanks to our highly evolved emotional radar, humans exist in a state of near-constant *distraction*. For our ancestors, distractions consisted of anything that might threaten their survival—things like running out of food, losing access to water, insufficient shelter, and predators. For most of human history, mitigating these threats was a full-time job. Given how precariously ancient hunter-gatherers clung to life, it's not surprising that they weren't big inventors or explorers. That doesn't mean they never explored or were curious about their world. Indeed, when the circumstances felt safe enough, that is exactly what they did. But since danger loomed constantly large, early humans did very little inventing or exploring.[3] It's no coincidence that all the major advances in human evolution—the compass, the printing press, the telegraph, the industrial revolution, antibiotics, etc.—came *after* basic survival resources were no longer in constant jeopardy. This is critically important for leaders to understand: **Human beings are hardwired to perform at their peak potential *only* when their most instinctive need—safety—is secure.**

Instinct is the reason that the flow state is so rare and so difficult to tap into. We may have evolved past physical threats to our existence, but there are still plenty of dangers that can and do

---

3 Dunn, Rob. "Anxious? Blame the Predators in Your Primate Family History." Slate Magazine, 15 Oct. 2012, https://slate.com/technology/2012/10/evolution-of-anxiety-humans-were-prey-for-predators-such-as-hyenas-snakes-sharks-kangaroos.html.

distract us from meeting our full potential. When *physical safety* is guaranteed, the highly evolved survival instincts of the human brain are directed toward ensuring *psychological safety*. As tribal, social creatures, this kind of safety was every bit as important to early humans as physical safety. As far as our brain is concerned, if our social system rejects us, we could die. Proof of this lies in the fact that the same part of the brain is responsible for assessing both physical and psychological safety. In both cases, it's the amygdala—the emotional part of the brain governed by subconscious instincts, impulses and intuition. When it comes to analyzing signals and making decisions, the amygdala makes virtually no distinction between physical and psychological safety. Neuroscience studies show that humans process social rejection in the brain's pain matrix, and the signature of social pain—getting fired, breakups or any other form of rejection—lasts even longer than that of physical pain, such as a punch in the gut.[4] Any perceived lack of psychological safety, therefore, has the exact same effect as a lack of physical safety: a *distraction* that prevents us from being completely present and unlocking our full potential. **The takeaway for leaders is that people will not—biologically *cannot*—perform to their full potential when they feel internally threatened, be-**

---

4   "The Pain of Social Rejection." Https://Www.Apa.Org, https://www.apa.org/monitor/2012/04/rejection.

cause threats are *distractions* that prevent them from entering a flow state.

Since we can't turn off the brain's overactive emotional radar, the key to tapping into group flow is to make sure we don't trip the alarms. That's where trust comes in. Trust is the the feeling of "I am safe," and it is the first signal we seek out to determine if we can open up or need to close down. Daniel Coyle, author of *The Culture Code,* calls these "belonging cues." Belonging cues are behaviors that create safe connections in groups. Their function is to answer the same ancient questions: *Am I safe here? Do I belong? Are there dangers lurking?* Belonging cues notify our hypervigilant brains that they can stop worrying about dangers and shift into connection mode.[5] When we feel safe, our brains down-regulate the activity of the hypothalamic pituitary adrenal axis, which lowers our stress response, and up-regulate our social engagement systems through the production of oxytocin and other prosocial hormones.[6] **In other words, trust triggers a physiological response that allows us to function at a higher level.** Trust is what allows groups to feel comfortable enough to set aside the shield of their defenses and become unselfconsciously involved in whatever

---

5   Coyle, Daniel. The Culture Code: The Secrets of Highly Successful Groups. Bantam Books, 2018.

6   Zak, Paul J., and Dan John Miller. Trust Factor. Unabridged edition, Brilliance Audio, 2017.

task they are performing. That's why the aforementioned group flow preconditions are so effective—they create the kind of trust our brains need to focus completely and totally on the here and now. Psychologists call them "flow triggers" but what they are actually "trust triggers." Here they are again:

1. **Familiarity:** People know one another and understand their tics and tendencies.
2. **Blending Egos:** Each person can submerge their ego needs into the group's.
3. **A Sense of Control:** Each member of the group feels in control, but still flexible.
4. **Shared Goals:** Everyone in the group is working towards the same end.
5. **Constant Communication:** There is a group version of immediate feedback.
6. **Equal Participation:** Everyone is involved and has roughly similar skill levels.
7. **Shared Group Risk:** Everyone has some skin in the game.
8. **Yes, And:** Conversations are additive, not combative.
9. **Close Listening:** You're paying complete attention to what is being said.
10. **Complete Concentration:** Total focus is on the right here, right now.

If flow is the number-one independent variable most commonly associated with extraordinary achievement, trust is the number-one independent variable most commonly associated with group flow. **Creating an environment conducive to flow is about creating an environment conducive to trust. If you are a leader trying to unlock the potential of your organization, creating this kind of environment is your responsibility—your *most important responsibility.*** Because it's as Stephen Covey said: "Without trust, we don't truly collaborate; we merely coordinate or, at best, cooperate. It is trust that transforms a group of people into a team."

A CRITICAL PARADIGM SHIFT

For most of us, this represents a major paradigm shift—research shows that only 49 percent of employees trust senior management, and only 28 percent believe CEOs are a credible source of information.[7] Such leaders no doubt think—as most of us do—that performance depends on measurable abilities like intelligence, skill and experience, not on subtle patterns of small behaviors. **To**

7　How the Best Leaders Build Trust by Stephen M. R. Covey @ LeadershipNow. https://www.leadershipnow.com/CoveyOnTrust.html#:~:text=Research%20shows%20 that%20only%2049,a%20credible%20source%20of%20information.&text=For%20 many%2C%20trust%20is%20intangible,or%20how%20to%20improve%20it.

get the most out of our people and organizations—to achieve a flow state—leaders need to fundamentally change how we think about trust. We must understand that when it comes to unlocking potential, nothing is more important. We must understand every person in our organization is constantly analyzing us for signals about our trustworthiness. We must understand that everything we say and do, no matter how seemingly trivial, is filed away as data and plotted on a subconscious graph that shows people how trustworthy we are. Until we do, we will continue to shoot ourselves in the foot. We'll keep choosing words, using body language and making decisions based on a misplaced faith in the supremacy of logic and reason. We'll continue starting conversations with a brusque, "Hey, listen…" and sending ominous "We need to talk" text messages with no regard for the damage we're doing to our team's performance.

Stephen Covey, author of *The 7 Habits of Highly Effective People*, calls such assaults on psychological safety "emotional bank account withdrawals." The emotional bank account works exactly like a regular bank account but instead of money, the currency is trust.[8] When we signal to someone that they are safe, we make deposits and our trust level grows; when we signal to someone

---

8   Covey, Stephen R. The 7 Habits of Highly Effective People: 30th Anniversary Edition. 4th edition, Simon & Schuster, 2020.

that they are not safe, we make withdrawals and our trust level decreases. In isolation, EBA withdrawals are not a big deal. But if they occur regularly they become extremely detrimental. **When teams don't completely trust each other, the lack of trust acts like a hidden tax on every transaction. Every communication, every interaction, every strategy and every decision is taxed, costing the organization money, time, energy and frustration.** Significant distrust doubles the cost of doing business and triples the time it takes to get things done. The end result is that a ceiling is placed on what the organization can achieve. This is consistent with research that shows that high-trust companies outperform low-trust companies by 286 percent.[9] That's because instead of a tax, high-trust organizations receive a *dividend* on every transaction that acts like a performance multiplier, enabling them to succeed in their communications, interactions and decisions, and to move with incredible speed.

Sound familiar? It should. That's flow. It's what happens when teams are on the same page about who they are, where they're going and how they're going to get there. To tap into it, leaders must lead with trust. Building an environment conducive to flow requires three different kinds of trust: 1. Teams need to trust each

---

9 Hornstein, Henry. Luss, Richard. Parker, Owen. The Watson Wyatt Human Capital Index and Company Performance: A definite impact on shareholder wealth. Watson Wyatt Worldwide. April 2002.

other, 2. They need to trust the organization, and 3. They need to trust the leader. The order of assembly, as we'll see, matters a great deal.

It starts with culture.

PART ONE

CULTURE

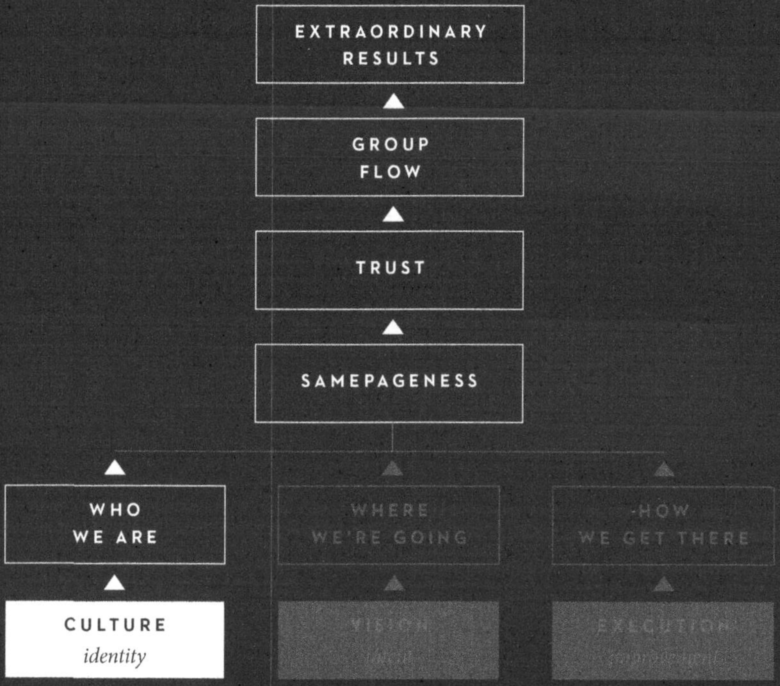
EXTRAORDINARY RESULTS
GROUP FLOW
TRUST
SAMEPAGENESS
WHO WE ARE
WHERE WE'RE GOING
HOW WE GET THERE
CULTURE
identity
VISION
EXECUTION

CULTURE
EATS STRATEGY
FOR BREAKFAST.

Peter Drucker

———

CULTURE

Of the three pillars of leadership, culture is by far the most powerful driver of group flow. This makes sense: Group flow is about teamwork, and that is essentially what culture is: a framework that determines how your team works together. The framework you build determines everything about how your people operate—their work ethic, commitment, vulnerability, growth, excellence, willingness to help, customer service, attention to detail, creativity—everything. The most successful cultures are the ones that facilitate incredible teamwork. **When it comes to building culture, this is the crux of the job: create an environment that enables the ultimate form of teamwork.**

The key to doing this, as we know from Chapter 1, is getting our teams to trust each other. It's a difficult task. In the past, both of my businesses oscillated between periods of dazzling teamwork and stretches seemingly devoid of it. By observing patterns during both of these periods, however, I honed in on the key variable at play: shared identity. The culture at CFNE and CompTrain is strongest when my teams are on the same page about who we are as an organization—when they know exactly what we stand for, what we believe in and how we conduct ourselves. Historically, the inverse has also been true. The most difficult times occured when my people veered off the same page; when I, as a leader, did not create enough "samepageness" about who we were as a group. As a result, teamwork was hampered. My people didn't share information as much. They skirmished over roles and responsibilities. There was less innovation, creative thinking and productivity. **Without a strong shared identity, groups of people struggle to act as a cohesive team.**

A shared identity produces strong culture because it creates a sense of belonging, a powerful signal of psychological safety that creates trust and allows teams to focus singularly on achieving their organization's goals. This is not how most leaders think about culture. We tend to think that culture is about keeping our team happy by making our organizations fun places to work, so we throw pizza parties and organize team happy hours and put foosball tables in the break room. But culture has little to do with fun. It's about samepageness about who the team is as a group. It's about identity.

Identity is based on what is important to us, our values. Our values define who we are, which in turn determine what social groups we join. There's a reason like-minded people become friends—studies show that individuals with similar notions about what is important in life trust each other more readily.[10] In a group setting, this kind of "familiarity" becomes a trust trigger; the first of ten preconditions for group flow we examined in the previous chapter. When someone is "one of us," we can let our guard down and be ourselves because, in our minds, our shared values significantly reduce potential threats. Simply put, like-minded people feel safe together. This, as we know, is the key to achieving a flow state. **Creating a sense of belonging in our organizations, therefore, is about building a strong organizational identity that will signal and attract like-minded people—the kind of people that naturally trust each other because they have similar ideas about what is important.**

This kind of "samepageness" is the linchpin of culture, and developing it is the focus of Part 1. In the next chapter, we'll talk about how to identify and define the beliefs that are most essential to your organization's success, codify these into a set of core values and actively use them to ensure you have the right people on

---

10   Kramer, Roderick M. "Rethinking Trust." Harvard Business Review, June 2009. hbr. org, https://hbr.org/2009/06/rethinking-trust.

your team. In the following chapter, we'll talk about how to develop principles based on your organizational identity and use them to operationalize the behaviors that are essential to your team's success. This, as we'll see, is the key to empowering our teams to consistently and independently act, decide and behave in ways that unlock the potential of organizations.

Culture, it must be said, is the most difficult pillar of leadership. And while getting it right is hard, it's not nearly as hard as getting it wrong. There's a reason culture is Part 1 of this book, before vision and execution. If we don't get the right people on board and help them trust each other, it won't matter how brilliant our vision is or how skilled we are at executing. Culture is a lot like rocket fuel in this sense: if you neglect it or misunderstand the chemistry, it's a dangerous bomb that will eventually destroy everything you build. But if you handle it deliberately and with great care, it can be an explosive propellant that will launch your organization to the moon.

**THOSE
WHO STAND FOR
NOTHING
FALL FOR
EVERYTHING.**

———

Alexander Hamilton

02

VALUES

I n 2010, I began hosting an annual CrossFit competition under the banner of CompTrain, my side hustle that catered to the competitive side of CrossFit. Over the years the event, cleverly named "The Competitor's Competition," began attracting Cross-Fitters from other gyms in the Boston area. By 2016, the competition hosted thousands of fans and featured a star-studded roster of perennial Games athletes. If you're familiar with CrossFit, you might know the event by a different name: The East Coast Championship. And while the ECC was no longer physically hosted at CompTrain HQ, my gym remained the de facto headquarters for the competition—both a staging ground and storage facility for all the equipment and signage that transformed Boston's World Trade Center into a CrossFit competition floor. The stacks of boxes grew throughout the year until finally, one week before the event, they were loaded onto a fleet of U-Haul trucks and shipped to the venue. It was during the 2016 ECC load-in that I first realized there was something seriously wrong with CFNE's culture.

It's early January and seasonably frigid, the kind of 7-degree day that makes even hardened New Englanders question their taste in geography. Harry Palley and I back up our rented U-Haul trucks to the gym's garage door, where the other half of the CompTrain staff—Trina Foster, Patrick Cummings and Ali Leblanc—grudgingly lift it, instantly lowering the gym's temperature by twenty degrees. The five of us begin the laborious process of lugging all the boxes from the back of the gym to the front and loading them into the trucks. If the number of boxes is any indication, the ECC is on track to have its biggest year yet.

At one point, I look around and realize how many CFNE coaches are at the gym. There are at least five. Because we have purposefully scheduled this load-in during the two-hour break between morning and afternoon classes, none of them is actually coaching. Some are training, some are eating, some are just hanging out. Yet no one—not a single person—offers to help us load the trucks. They just watch us load box after box. It never occurs to them to help. Why should they? They work for CrossFit New England, not CompTrain. Loading ECC stuff isn't their job. Strictly speaking, no one is doing anything wrong. And yet, it doesn't feel right. To me, it feels horribly wrong.

This isn't the kind of team I want to have. My vision is excellence. I want CFNE to be the best CrossFit gym in the world—a huge, ambitious goal. To stand any chance of making it a reality, CFNE needs a culture of *teamwork*, the kind of place where people go above and beyond at every opportunity not because they are expected to but because they *want* to. The kind of team that would drop everything to help their teammates, regardless of whether it was "their job" or not. Up until this moment, I thought we *did* have that kind of team. Clearly, I was mistaken.

If I'm being honest with myself, this isn't new information. The truth is that CFNE isn't the shining beacon of affiliate achievement most in the community think it is. Our success at the CrossFit Games (our team won the affiliate cup in 2010 and continues to contend for the podium year after year) suggests a culture of excellence, but it's a mirage. The real CFNE is the gym I see every day, whose defining feature by 2016 is a bloated staff of extremely talented but wildly unproductive coaches. No one on my team, it seems, is eager to do anything other than coach a class or two and train themselves for their next competition. I try to delegate, with little success. Unsure of what to do about this and anxious about things falling through the cracks, I step into the voids. I'm working sixty- to eighty-hour weeks just to keep up. My employees, meanwhile, are enjoying the opposite experience—they are paid handsomely for a minimal amount of work. Not surprisingly, very few of the coaches I hire ever leave. To most people, low turnover is considered a metric of success, a sign that employees are happy. After the ECC load-in, I begin to see it as a sign that we have become deeply complacent—a world away from the kind of team I need to help CFNE's members live healthier, happier, more fulfilled lives. And I know it has to change.

A few weeks after the 2016 ECC, I gather the entire coaching staff together for a meeting, which takes place at the picnic tables outside the gym. "We don't have enough turnover," I begin bluntly. Ten faces stare back at me blankly. I continue, "Most of you have been here for three, four or even five years. During that time, I haven't done my job of communicating my vision, training and developing you guys, upholding standards or fulfilling my role as a leader." I tell my team that we have not been acting in line with our values and starting today, that is going to change. "From now on, I am going to do a better job of leading, managing and creating the team I know we can be. I realize that what I'm going to be asking of you may be different from what you signed up for or what we've done in the past, so I completely understand if you'd like to try working somewhere else." I look meaningfully from person to person, so that they know I am speaking directly to them. "In a year from now, I think you'll be surprised at how few people are still here at this table." After laying out expectations, I watch my staff walk solemnly back to the gym. I know they're shaken by my talk.

I was shaken too, but for different reasons. I didn't understand how this had happened. It wasn't like I didn't understand the importance of culture. I did. I read all the books: *Work Rules* (Laszlo Bock), *The Culture Code* (Daniel Coyle), *Delivering Happiness* (Tony Hsieh), *Leaders Eat Last* (Simon Sinek), *The Culture Quotient* (Gregory Besner). From the beginning, I had a very clear idea about the kind of culture I wanted to cultivate at my gym. I understood that the best organizations adhere to a set of core values that define who they are and what they stand for. I spent a lot of time trying to put my finger on the values that would produce what CFNE needed: great *teammates.*

The first one is "humility." Great team players don't have big egos or concerns about status. They are quick to point out the contributions of others and generally don't seek attention for themselves. They define success collectively, not individually. The second one is "hunger." Hungry people are always looking for more—more to do, more to learn, more responsibility. They rarely have to be pushed to work harder because they're self-motivated and diligent. They're always thinking about the next step and the next opportunity. The last one is "people smarts." Emotionally intelligent people have good common sense about other people. They tend to know what is happening in the group and how to deal effectively with others. They ask good questions, listen to what others are saying and stay engaged in conversations. I borrowed these core values straight from Patrick Lencioni, but it's a theft he encourages in his book, *The Ideal Team Player*: "Any leader who wants to make teamwork a reality should find and/or develop people who are hungry, humble and people smart."[11] Like Lencioni, I was convinced that great teamwork was not possible without all three virtues. That's why the 2016 ECC load-in hit me like a punch in the gut—the complete lack of teamwork shattered any illusion that my values had taken hold.

YOU REAP WHAT YOU SOW

In retrospect, it's not surprising that my values did not translate into anything resembling teamwork or group flow. Results, after all, are simply the product of *actions*—you reap what you sow, as they say. And in the seven years since I opened CFNE, I had taken very little action to convert my values into an organizational identity. In other words, I was not *intentional* about building a culture. Most leaders aren't, for one of two reasons: We either don't have time to think about culture because we're consumed with the day-to-day realities of running our organizations, or we don't understand what culture really is, believing that it's about creating

---

11 Lencioni, Patrick M. The Ideal Team Player: How to Recognize and Cultivate The Three Essential Virtues. 1st edition, Jossey-Bass, 2016.

a fun, happy place to work. In my case, it was a combination of both—which is why, by 2016, the culture at CFNE was so far removed from the one that existed in my mind. This is to be expected. When we aren't intentional about what we're trying to create, we have no control over what ultimately emerges. And when it comes to culture, something *will* emerge. All organizations have culture; just because we didn't build it on purpose doesn't mean it's not there. Culture is nothing more than the sum of the actions, decisions and behaviors of the people who operate within it. Think of culture like a jungle—it will grow whether you tend to it or not. If you want something specific to take root, you have to get in there and cultivate it intentionally.

Building culture intentionally starts with identifying the beliefs that underpin your organizational identity, then codifying them into a set of core values. I had done both. To make CFNE the best CrossFit gym in the world, I knew I needed coaches who craved feedback ("humble"), who would strive for constant improvement ("hungry") and who possessed high levels of emotional intelligence ("people smart"). So why hadn't my values taken hold and produced the team I wanted? *Because I stopped there.* The problem at CFNE wasn't that I didn't know what I was trying to get my staff to buy into. It was that I hadn't taken any steps to actually help them buy into it. The disconnect was in the way I was using my core values; or rather, not using them. Up to that point, my efforts to share my core values with my team consisted of hanging a poster about them in the CFNE office, sending out a handful of emails defining them in more detail and talking about them during the occasional staff meeting. This, I discovered, is about as effective as brushing your teeth without toothpaste—you're going through the motions but not accomplishing anything. That's because simply hearing something rarely results in a change in behavior. In order for core values to have any impact on organizational culture, you have to actually use them to lead. And I was not.

CREATING AN ORGANIZATIONAL IDENTITY

If you don't lead with your core values, you won't achieve your desired organizational identity. Identity is what allows us to signal and attract like-minded people—the kind of people who naturally trust each other because they have similar ideas about what is important.[12] Author Idowu Koyenikan said it best: "There is immense power when a group of people with similar interests gets together to work toward the same goals." **This is the fundamental task of culture building: getting the right people on our team**

---

12 Druskat, Vanessa Urch, and Steven B. Wolff. "Building the Emotional Intelligence of Groups." Harvard Business Review, Mar. 2001. hbr.org, https://hbr.org/2001/03/building-the-emotional-intelligence-of-groups.

and making sure the wrong people don't remain on the team.
If you want to make an amazing meal, you have to cook with the
right food.

If you don't use your core values to lead, you're going to end
up with the wrong people. By "wrong," I don't mean individuals
who are bad people or bad at their jobs. By "wrong," I mean people
who don't share our values or want the same things as we do out
of work and life. Value alignment is important because individuals with similar notions about what is important in life trust each
other more readily.[13] This is why "familiarity" is one of ten "trust
triggers" we examined in Chapter 1. We are hardwired to judge
whether someone is more like or unlike us; the more "unlike"
we determine them to be, the less time we want to spend around
them. When someone is "one of us," by contrast, we can let our
guard down and be ourselves because our shared values significantly reduce potential threats. We need like-minded people on
our teams because like-minded people feel safe together. And this
increases our ability to access a flow state.

When a group becomes that cohesive, it develops a strong
culture—people share the same values and norms, and believe in
them intensely. But there's a fine line between having a strong culture and operating like a cult, where conformity is valued over all

---

13   Godin, Seth. Tribes: We Need You to Lead Us. 1st edition, Portfolio, 2008.

else. That kind of groupthink, of course, is not an asset. "Yes men" are useless. Diversity of all types—gender, socioeconomic background, race, creed—is essential. We need people who think differently than we do, that bring different perspectives and opinions. Samepageness is not the same thing as sameness. We want both creative and analytical thinking on our teams, and those willing to challenge our strategies and assumptions.

What we can't have are people whose values clash. If you have ever dated or been married to another human being, you almost certainly know from experience why this is problematic. For most people, the goal of dating and marriage is to find a life partner—someone who shares your worldview and wants the same things out of life. As individuals, we understand this intuitively. If you ardently want to have children but your partner doesn't, the relationship will face constant friction. If you cherish the lives of animals but your partner is really into hunting, you're going to have issues. It's not a matter of right or wrong; it's about harmony. Dating apps know how important this is and have built in all kinds of filters into their software to help users find people who share their values. If smoking is a dealbreaker, for example, you can edit your preferences so that smokers never even appear in your feed. The dating app Hinge advertises itself as "the app that's designed to be deleted." Clearly, the company understands that value alignment is the only way to make good on that promise.

It's no less important in an organizational setting. Imagine if Planned Parenthood hired someone who believes, as many people do, that life begins at conception. To this person, abortion is tantamount to murder. In an organization like Planned Parenthood, that belief is going to create friction at literally every decision point. A team made up of individuals who believe fervently in a woman's right to choose is going to have an impossible time trusting this employee. The misalignment in values becomes a constant *distraction* that will preoccupy the entire team and prevent them from tapping into group flow.

This is obviously an extreme example, but friction can be created with far subtler value misalignment. And so it did at CFNE in 2016. I needed humble coaches who wanted to improve and embraced feedback as an opportunity to do it, but I never talked about this with prospective employees so I ended up with people who either shied away from feedback or scoffed at it. I needed the kind of people who naturally went above and beyond, but I never set this expectation so I ended up with coaches who were comfortable with "good enough." I needed people who would go out of their way to treat every CFNE member as though they were wearing a sign that said "make me feel special," but I almost exclusively hired talented athletes whom I liked, so what I got was a bunch of really cool people who were more interested in their own training than helping the members improve or contributing to the team.

HOW TO LEAD WITH CORE VALUES

The key to creating a shared organizational identity, argues Patrick Lencioni, is to make your values mean something: "[If] they're going to really take hold in your organization, your core values need to be integrated into every employee-related process—hiring methods, performance management systems, criteria for promotions and rewards, and even dismissal policies. From the first interview to the last day of work, employees should be constantly reminded that core values form the basis for every decision the company makes."[14] Most of these decisions fit into one of four categories: Hire, Fire, Reward or Review. Using your values to make these kinds of important personnel decisions is a key to bringing them to life—it's how values become a shared identity. The key to building culture is to prove, through your actions, that those values actually matter. Using them to hire, fire, reward and review is a strong way to do it.

Hire

The first big opportunity to do this at CFNE came midway through 2016. As I predicted during the Table Turnover Talk, my gym was experiencing a quiet exodus. Halfway through the year, several coaches had moved on, and so, after five years with practically

---

14 Lencioni, Patrick M. "Make Your Values Mean Something." Harvard Business Review, July 2002. hbr.org, https://hbr.org/2002/07/make-your-values-mean-something.

zero turnover, CFNE suddenly needed to hire four new coaches.

The key to hiring high-trust people is value alignment. As leaders, our job when recruiting people to join our teams is to find talented people who share our organizational identity. When hiring, we should think of ourselves as defenders of the culture. We are Heimdall, the mythological watchman of Asgard who guards the bridge between Asgard and all other realms. In practice, this amounts to essentially trying to scare candidates off with your organization's core values. The more up front we are about our values, the more likely we are to end up with people who genuinely share them. This is where culture starts—the first interview is the first on-boarding session.

Whenever I interview potential coaches, hammering on our values is my number-one priority. After the niceties and all the normal background questions, I deliver what I have taken to calling the "Core Values Speech." I start by laying out CFNE's values—humble, hungry and people smart—then explain what each one looks like in practice. The first one is humility. To us, I explain, humility is about recognizing that none of us individually has all the answers. I say, "I realize that this might be different from where you're coming from, but at CFNE we share ideas and give each other feedback *a lot*. If you feel like you might not enjoy radical candor and getting coached all the time, you're probably going to feel uncomfortable here." This, I emphasize, is not a matter of right or wrong; it's a matter of cultural fit. I want my team to genuinely enjoy being at work, and that's hard to do if you don't enjoy constant feedback.

The same is true of our second core value: hunger. To us, hunger is about work ethic. Our team is made up of people who *love* to work—they'd rather be at work than at home. Again, I'm extremely frank about expectations. "If you're the kind of person who counts down the minutes until you can leave, you're going to stick out like a sore thumb here," I say. "This team works sixty- to eighty-hour weeks *for fun.*"

I continue in this manner—quite literally trying to scare the candidate off—while laying out the last value: people smart. To us, I explain, this is about positivity. At CFNE, we don't believe in whining, complaining or making excuses. We literally have white bracelets that we all wear as a reminder—I reach for my right wrist and give my own well-worn bracelet a snap—and if one of us accidently complains, someone calls them out and we snap our bracelet. "I know this isn't the norm in most places," I tell them. "If you're the kind of person that normally complains about politics, the weather or other people, that's cool. Plenty of people do. But you're going to stick out at a place like CFNE. It's going to be uncomfortable, and I don't want that for you. I want you to *love* being at work. I want you to feel at home here."

I conclude the core values speech by reiterating to potential employees that this isn't the right or wrong way to run a business.

It's just the way we run our business. "How well you gel with our culture is going to shape your experience here," I tell them.

While intentionally trying to scare candidates away from your organization might seem counterintuitive, it's actually the best possible way to ensure the right people get on the bus. A lot of potential coaches take in my core values speech wearing expressions of barely concealed panic. They're probably thinking, "Uh, that sounds really hard. That doesn't sound fun at all." This is exactly the goal—to identify the "wrong" people and allow them to self-select out of the interview process. The people who are a good fit, on the other hand, hear the exact same pitch and have a completely different reaction. In 2016, it was a potential coach from Washington, D.C., named Elizabeth. As I delivered the core values speech, her expression was barely concealed *excitement*. When I was done, I continued to pry. "You seem to like D.C. and have a good thing going down there," I observed. "What about CFNE makes you consider moving up here and essentially starting over?" Beth shrugged. "I taught myself to coach by reading the CrossFit Journal and watching YouTube videos," she said. "I'm out of content. I need someone to coach *me* now." Her answer said a lot about her hunger and humility. This was a coach who wanted feedback so badly she was willing to uproot her entire life to get it. We hired Elizabeth at the end of her interview and she moved to Boston a few weeks later.

Fire

Getting the right people on the bus is the fun part of culture building—one of the few fun parts, in truth. Done correctly, leading with core values inflicts more pain than pleasure. Along with getting the right people on the bus, it's also about letting the wrong people *off* the bus. As leaders, we are responsible for this too. Removing someone from the team is always a tough decision, but it's an important way to reinforce our organizational identity and core values. If someone isn't a character fit, their continued presence undermines the team's culture. By 2016, this had been the case at CFNE for at least four years. Fortunately, the Table Turnover Talk had prompted a few of these coaches to get off the bus voluntarily, but not all of them. By the fall of 2016, at least one remained, a coach named Jamie.* Unfortunately, it only takes one person to undermine trust and block group flow—one bad apple is enough to poison the whole bunch. It wouldn't matter how "right" my new hires were if I allowed even one wrong person to stay on. With that in mind, I made the difficult decision to let Jamie go.

While our personal feelings can often make these decisions seem complicated, value misalignment should always be black and white. It doesn't matter how great a performer someone is; if they don't embody all your values, their continued presence is un-

---

* Not her real name.

dermining the culture—which is to say, group trust, and thereby the group's ability to tap into the performance-enhancing power of flow. This is not to say, of course, that performance doesn't matter. A shared organizational identity will unlock potential, but it can't conjure it. The "right" people are great character fits who are also great performers. A serious deficit in either area is grounds for termination. By firing Jamie in 2016, I signaled to the rest of the team that performance never trumps values. As much as I hated doing it, it lent further weight to CFNE's values, pulling them off the poster in the office and inserting them into the oxygen.

Reward

From a leadership perspective, so much of building culture is about showing what matters to you. Hiring is about getting the right people on the bus. Firing is about letting the wrong people off the bus. But it's just as important to *keep* the right people on the bus. As leaders, we do this by rewarding the people who embody our values. Institutions get the behaviors they reward. The problem is that, as leaders, we tend to have lopsided metrics for reviewing our people. We have a million metrics to measure someone's performance and virtually none to measure someone's trustworthiness and intangible contributions to the team. And so we end up rewarding toxicity in our organizations, which eventually undermines what our teams are capable of.

As I began overhauling my hiring process, I sought to emulate successful models of high-performing groups. There is probably no better example than the U.S. Naval Special Warfare Development Group. Most people know it by another name: SEAL Team Six. The criteria the Navy uses to select people for the highest-performing team on the planet doesn't look anything like the criteria most organizations use to hire people. DEVGRU, as it's known within the Navy, plots candidates on a graph in which one axis represents performance and the other represents trust.[15]

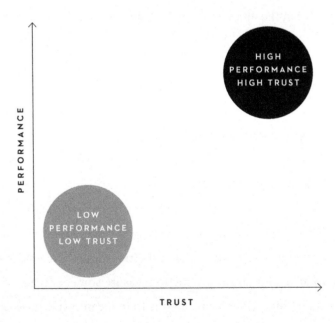

15 What Makes the Highest Performing Teams in the World | Simon Sinek. www.youtube.com, https://www.youtube.com/watch?v=zP9jpxitfb4.

Of course nobody wants the person in the bottom left of the graph—the low-performance/low-trust person. Everybody wants the person in the top right of the graph—the high-performance/high-trust person. But what the Navy has learned is that the person in the top left—the high-performance/low-trust person—is a toxic team member. **The highest-performing organization on the planet would rather have a medium performer with high trust or even a low performer with high trust over a high-performing person with low trust.** This is how important trust is to culture, and thereby team performance.

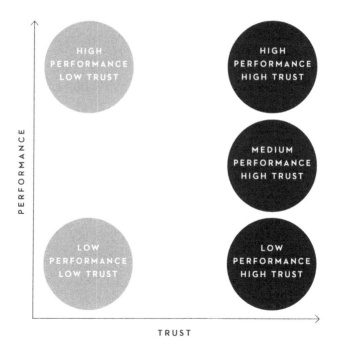

It's unbelievably easy to find high-performance/low-trust people. As Simon Sinek says in his book, *Infinite Game*, simply go to any team and ask, "Who's the asshole?" Everyone on the team will point to the same person. Conversely, if you go to any team and say, "Who do you trust more than anybody else?" the entire team will also all point to one person.[16] That person is the most valuable member of the team *because they are creating an environment for everybody else to succeed.* They may not be the highest individual performer, but the trust that they inspire contributes something much more important: the kind of teamwork that leads to group flow.

For the last thirteen years, this person at CFNE has been Harry Palley. Harry was the first employee I ever hired, back in 2008, and by 2016 he was still the personification of what it meant to be humble, hungry and people smart. He was also beloved by the members, who bent over backwards to try and be more like him. In that sense, Harry was a cultural linchpin—his very presence inspired our members to be healthier, happier people. I couldn't afford to lose Harry, ever. I knew, however, that he wouldn't be content as CFNE's head coach forever. A growth-minded person like Harry is constantly looking for new challenges, and as he got older, I knew he would also be looking for the financial stability to put down roots. CFNE, unfortunately, had a ceiling on both—the

---

16   Sinek, Simon. The Infinite Game. Penguin Random House, 2019.

head coach position was the most senior role in the organization and the gym simply didn't have the resources to award substantial raises every year. If I wanted to keep Harry, I was going to have to find new opportunities for growth that would also give him the financial incentive he needed to stick around. In 2016, I found the solution: CompTrain. What had begun as a pet project in 2010 was, largely because of Harry, morphing into something much bigger. It was Harry's idea to expand and monetize the programming, which he did single-handedly by creating and running CompTrain Masters. Recognizing the potential for growth, I made him co-owner of the company, an equal partner in whatever success we were able to achieve going forward. Thankfully for both CFNE and CompTrain, it worked. All these years later, Harry remains my longest-tenured employee and one of my greatest friends.

Review

Ensuring that only the right people are on the bus demands constant vigilance. Leaders need to consistently review their people using an assessment tool that recognizes both performance and trust. Prior to 2016, performance had been my only criteria. Starting in 2016, I began using each of CFNE's three core values to assess members of the team in terms of their trustworthiness. It's a format I've used for years, and it has been mostly effective at helping to ensure that only the right people stay on the bus. The one-on-one nature of any assessment, however, is problematic. Personal biases, for example—be they favorable or unfavorable—have occasionally skewed core value assessments and led to the wrong people being allowed to remain on the bus. To eliminate these kinds of blind spots in CFNE's review process, I implemented a new method of assessing team member trustworthiness. Instead of managers assessing their people in terms of how they embody our values, we now put that question in the hands of the entire team. The idea is that everyone on the team reviews everybody else according to how they exemplify our core values. They are sent the following survey and asked to (anonymously, of course) rank their teammates across thirty different criteria that fall under either "Humble," "Hungry" or "People Smart." This survey represents one half of their review, the other half being their actual skills, performance and results.

TEAMMATE PERFORMANCE REVIEW

How often does **[Employee Name]** live up to our core values?

1 = Rarely   2 = Sometimes   3 = Most of the time   4 = Almost always

HUMBLE

	1	2	3	4
Is coachable	○	○	○	○
Knows it's about team wins, not personal achievement	○	○	○	○
Admits & takes responsibility for shortcomings and mistakes	○	○	○	○
Listens wholeheartedly to others' ideas	○	○	○	○
Willingly takes on lower-level work for the good of the team	○	○	○	○
Happily lets others have the spotlight	○	○	○	○
Sees feedback as a chance to learn, not as a judgment of their performance	○	○	○	○
Tries to learn something from everyone	○	○	○	○
Excitedly supports decisions, even if they don't get their way	○	○	○	○
Embraces change	○	○	○	○

HUNGRY

	1	2	3	4
Works hard & gets stuff done	○	○	○	○
Takes on more responsibility than is required	○	○	○	○
Takes action to get better, improve and grow	○	○	○	○
Is responsible—takes ownership, does it well & does it fast	○	○	○	○
Eagerly pushes the boundaries of excellence	○	○	○	○
Is curious about how to improve everything	○	○	○	○
Happily takes on challenging tasks	○	○	○	○
Is one of the hardest workers I know	○	○	○	○
Shows fanatical attention to detail	○	○	○	○
Passionately contributes ideas	○	○	○	○

PEOPLE SMART

	1	2	3	4
Is a joy to be around	○	○	○	○
Seeks to understand others	○	○	○	○
Never whines, complains or makes excuses	○	○	○	○
Stays level-headed; not overly emotional	○	○	○	○
Shows empathy to members and teammates	○	○	○	○
Is an attentive, sincere & active listener	○	○	○	○
Communicates clearly & to the point without unnecessary details	○	○	○	○
Adjusts behavior & communication style to fit the conversation/relationship	○	○	○	○
Uses body language to enhance belonging (smiles, nods, eye contact, etc.)	○	○	○	○
Is people smart—has high emotional intelligence	○	○	○	○

This method is powerful because we are essentially reviewing the employee and prescribing the behaviors of the ideal team player at the same time. The knowledge that their performance review will be based partly on their peers' assessment of them is an incentive to be a great team player year round. This takes away much of the anxiety surrounding performance reviews. The reason reviews are usually the source of fear is because people don't know what to expect. By asking our team to assess one another based on our core values, we are essentially giving them the answers to the test in advance—every employee at CFNE and CompTrain knows exactly how to earn a great performance review. When people know what to expect, they gain psychological safety. This, as we know, allows them to spend less time thinking about how to protect themselves and more time focusing on the task at hand, which is essential to group flow.

•

As human beings, we are hardwired to protect ourselves by avoiding danger and seeking safety. The best place to be is around others who make us feel safe and protected. Strong relationships lead to trust, which is what enables extraordinary results. To foster trust, we as leaders need to create a culture in which trust is the defining feature. We do this by using our organizational identity to determine who joins the team and who stays on the team—by hiring, firing, rewarding and reviewing team members in terms of value alignment. A shared organizational identity is the secret sauce that separates great organizations from the rest because it creates the kind of belonging among teams that triggers trust. When we use our core values to lead, we create "samepageness" among our teams about who we are as a group, which leads to group flow and all its performance benefits.

In 2015, a paper published in the *European Journal of Management* explains why talking about our values with our teams is a critical part of making them part of organizational culture. According to the data, companies who changed their core values over time outperformed firms who kept theirs stable.[17] At first, this seems jarringly counterintuitive; it seems completely at odds with Patrick Lenceoni's argument that effective values must be integrated into every system that touches people. How are you supposed to integrate your values into your systems if you're always tweaking them? This line of thinking, however, assumes that a shared identity comes from the words we choose to define our values. But as the research suggests, the power isn't in the words—it's in the *conversation*. Companies that tweak their values are having conversations about them—lots and lots of conversations. These con-

---

17 Jonsen, Karsten, et al. Evaluating Espoused Values: Does Articulating Values Pay Off? European Management Journal, Oct. 2015, pp. 332-40, https://www.sciencedirect.com/science/article/pii/S0263237315000444.

versations reflect a deeply ingrained desire to reform and improve and *that* is what drives superior performance. The implication is that culture is not a one-off purchase; it's a living, growing thing. Core values may be the seeds of a shared organizational identity, but sustained conversation is the fertilizer that will make them grow. The best leaders don't wrestle with their organizational identity by themselves, they get their teams to wrestle it with them. Together, they constantly redefine their values and rigorously articulate their meanings.

NEVER TELL PEOPLE
HOW TO DO THINGS.
TELL THEM WHAT TO DO
AND THEY WILL SURPRISE
YOU WITH THEIR
INGENUITY.

General George Patton

03

CODIFY

By the end of 2016, CFNE had successfully developed an organizational identity by using core values to make decisions about the team—who joined, who stayed, who had to go. I was hopeful but skeptical. I resolved to withhold celebration until I saw a seismic shift in my team's behavior. I remember the first time I knew we were on the right track. It was a Thursday morning in January of 2017. The workout of the day at CFNE was "Filthy 50," a classic CrossFit benchmark:

"Filthy 50"

For Time:
50 Box Jumps (20")
50 Jumping Pull-Ups
50 Kettlebell Swings (35/25#)
50 Walking Lunges
50 Knees-to-Elbows
50 Push Press (45/35#)
50 Back Extensions
50 Wallballs (20/14#)
50 Burpees
50 Double-Unders

Everything that makes "Filthy 50" fun for CrossFit athletes makes it challenging for CrossFit coaches. It takes almost military levels of organizational precision to safely and effectively put twenty-plus people through a ten-part chipper in a sixty-minute class. CFNE pulls it off by employing a very precise floor setup. All the boxes get pulled out and grouped together in the back of the room. We designate stations for jumping pull-ups by lining up stacks of bumper plates under the rig. The kettlebells, barbells and wallballs are arranged neatly in sections that correspond with the flow of the workout and are organized by weight. Working quickly, it takes one person about forty-five minutes to get everything in place. The task of doing all of this falls on whoever coaches the 5:30 a.m. class, CFNE's first class of the day.

On this particular morning, it's Conor Nugent. He arrives at four thirty and sets about arranging hundreds of pounds of gym equipment. He is no more than five boxes in when the door swings open and Dan DeLomba, a recently hired coaching intern, walks in. Conor looks at his watch. It's 4:39 a.m. *Why is Dan here so early?* Conor knows Dan works the front desk on Thursday mornings, but front-desk shifts don't start until 5:15 a.m. And it's not like Dan lives close by—he commutes from Danvers, Massachusetts, for-ty-five minutes away. Conor does some quick math. To be here this early, Dan would have had to leave at 3:50 a.m., which meant he probably woke up around ... 3:30 a.m.? *Whoa. Why would anyone show up for a front-desk shift so early?* But Dan didn't arrive early to work the front desk. He's here because he knows how labor inten-sive the "Filthy 50" setup is, and he doesn't want Conor to have to do it all by himself. He walks over and begins grabbing boxes as if there is nothing unusual about this. Conor laughs, imagining how much coffee Dan consumed on the drive here to be functioning so early. "How you doing?" he asks. Dan gives a sleepy smile, shakes his head softly and says evenly, "I'm so fucking good right now."

To almost everyone who heard about this, it was just a funny CFNE story. Had an outsider been there to witness it, it would have probably seemed like the most natural thing in the world. When I heard about it, I felt like I won the lottery. That kind of thing would have *never* happened at CFNE a year ago. It was *anything* but natural. What happened in the gym that morning was the result of intentionally developed core values designed to produce exactly this kind of behavior. Dan's actions were incredibly specific: He arrived early to help his teammate. *Hunger.* He did so at great personal inconvenience. *Humility.* And not only did he not complain about it (even when given a chance), but he somehow managed to radiate positive body language the whole time. *People smart.* No one told Dan to do any of those things. He just did them. I began to feel confident that our core values would continue to drive my team's actions, decisions and behavior.

And they did. Some of the time.

The rest of the time, however, our values seemed to have no impact on their behavior and decision-making. The following week, for example, Dan was back squatting in CFNE's side room in between classes. I happened to be walking by when he was approached by a member, a woman named Susan, in between sets. Oblivious to the fact that Dan was in the middle of his own workout, Susan asked if he could give her some feedback on her pull-ups. Dan smiled, genial and polite as ever. "Absolutely," he said. "Just give me five minutes to finish lifting, then I'll be right there." True to his word, Dan emerged from the side room a few minutes later to work with Susan, who was visibly grateful for the free personal training. Nevertheless, I was disappointed. The correct way to handle that situation would have been for Dan to drop everything and immediately help Susan when she asked, regardless of his own workout. Being people smart is about treating people as though there is a sign around their neck that says, "Make me feel special." By opting to finish lifting before helping Susan, Dan—someone I knew to be sensationally people smart—had made the wrong decision.

Throughout 2017, CFNE was full of these dichotomies. It was frustrating to me. I had gone to great lengths to make sure that the right people—and only the right people—were on my team. And they were. They were humble, hungry and people smart, spectacularly so at times. But other times, I was having to practically hold their hands. As a result, I was spending a lot of time—too much time—micromanaging my team. Every week, I met one on one with every employee to discuss their progress on the projects they were currently working on and help them identify and plan future projects.

STACKING GOOD HABITS

As a coach, I understood why this was problematic. One of the things I am constantly talking about with my athletes—both Cross-Fit Games competitors and regular members at CFNE—is habits. The key to maximizing athletic performance is to create good habits and break bad habits. This is because success is a matter of stacking up good actions, decisions and behaviors over and over and over. Achievement isn't the result of a few big actions; it's the sum of thousands of small ones. The same, I knew, was true in business. But if my gym was going to become everything I imagined it could be, my habits weren't the only ones that mattered. **Unlocking your organization's full potential requires every single person on the team to stack good actions, decisions and behaviors.**

As 2016 became 2017, this was inconsistently the case at CFNE. My new staff was earnest and hardworking and wanted to do the right thing, but for some reason, they often missed the mark. I wished there was a way to download my brain into a PDF document I could share with my team—not because I wanted them to be just like me, but because stacking good habits would be so much easier if everyone understood the mental template I used to decide how to handle any given situation. Obviously, the notion of PDFing my brain was ridiculous. Or was it? My problem, I realized, wasn't that my team couldn't read my mind. It was that I hadn't given them a framework to make good decisions on their own. The more I thought about it, the more obvious it seemed. Of course a handful of core values—three words—are not enough information for anyone, even the "right" people, to instinctively know what the "right" thing is in any given situation. I had effectively invited my team to play Monopoly without explaining the rules of the game—they

CODIFY

were rolling the dice and going around the board, but didn't know what to do when they landed on the various squares. I didn't need to export my brain. I needed to teach my team the rules of the game.

THE OTHER HALF OF IDENTITY

In an organizational setting, the rules of the game are called principles. Principles are fundamental truths that can be used to decide how to act, behave and make decisions. They are the next step to operationalizing our core values. **Because while core values are an important part of culture, they are only one half of a strong organizational identity.** Shared values will ensure that you get the right people on the bus, but they won't consistently drive the kind of actions, decisions and behaviors that are essential to your organization's success. For that, leaders need principles—the second half of organizational identity. To understand why, let's return to the Planned Parenthood example from the previous chapter. Obviously, a passionately pro-life person is going to clash with the kind of pro-choice people who are drawn to an organization like Planned Parenthood. By recruiting people who share PP's belief in a woman's right to choose, the organization can keep the "wrong" people outside of the organization. But how does a woman's right to choose help the "right" people make decisions about how to behave? It doesn't. Once you're in the building, core values don't provide a lot of direction.

That's why principles are so important. They are rules of thumb that people can use to act, behave and decide in ways that best advance the organization's goals. In nature, these are known as *heuristics*: a kind of mental shortcut that eases the cognitive load of making a decision. That's exactly what principles are—mental shortcuts that provide guidance by creating if/then scenarios in vivid, memorable ways. Military rules of engagement are a useful example. Rules of engagement delineate when, where, how and against whom military force may be used. "Do not target or strike hospitals," for example, is a common combat principle. During the Iraq War, one of the United States's rules of engagement was, "Do not target enemy infrastructure or lines of communication unless necessary for self-defense." As a result, soldiers in these situations behaved in specific ways without being micromanaged. If Marines engaged enemies near a bridge, for example, they did everything they could to disable or disrupt the bridge without destroying it.

This concept is just as practical in the real world. If health is one of your core values, for example, a prescriptive principle might be, "Eat real food, not too much, mostly plants." With a single eight-word catchphrase, a somewhat vague core value becomes a foolproof formula you can use to navigate practically any conceivable dietary situation. You don't need to Google it or ask your CrossFit coach because *you have a template to figure out the answer yourself.* Principles are the essence of the oft-quoted proverb: "Give a man a fish and you feed him for a day. Teach a man to fish and you feed him for a lifetime." Leadership, from a culture standpoint, is not about feeding your teams—it's about teaching them how to feed themselves.

As leaders, it is essential that we utilize principles to make our core values actionable. Without principles, you are essentially in charge of making every single decision in the organization. The result is a kind of *Groundhog Day* existence in which we find ourselves dealing with the same problems over and over again. As frustrating as this is for leaders, the effect it has on our organizational culture is much more damaging. When we don't give people a framework for how to conduct themselves, every situation requires a guess.[18]

Without principles, this is essentially what we are asking our teams to do—guess. The resulting uncertainty represents an emotional bank account withdrawal; trust is eroded because our people lack a sense of control over their performance. Not knowing how to succeed is stressful and distracting. This explains why a sense of control is one of the ten preconditions for group flow: "Each member of the group feels in control, but still flexible." This is exactly what principles do. They illuminate the best course of action while giving people the freedom to respond based on the circumstances, which are often similar but never exactly the same. Principles help us strike a balance between two extremes: autonomy and microman-

---

18   Dalio, Ray. Principles. Later prt. edition, Simon & Schuster, 2017.

aging. I tend to default toward autonomy, but micromanagement is probably more common. It is just as ineffective, for the opposite reason—too much structure robs people of the freedom they need to feel ownership of their work. This sense of control helps create trust among teams and reduces the kind of distractions—anxiety, doubt, fear—that prevent groups from operating in a flow state.

DEFINING YOUR PRINCIPLES

Since principles are a derivative of organizational values, creating them is essentially a matter of defining your core values. The trick is to come up with definitions that are simple, action-oriented and forthright: "Create fun and a little weirdness" (Zappos). "Talk less, do more" (IDEO). "Work hard, be nice" (KIPP). "Pound the rock" (San Antonio Spurs). "Leave the jersey in a better place" (New Zealand All Blacks). "Create raves for guests" (Danny Meyer's restaurants). Each of these examples share an action-based clarity. They aren't gentle suggestions so much as clear reminders, crisp nudges in the direction we, as leaders, want the group to go.

This is exactly what my team needed in 2017. I started by jotting down every definition I could think of for "Humble," "Hungry" and "People Smart." It was a long list. By the time I was done, I had close to twenty statements for each core value—too many. To reduce the list, I decided to enlist my team. During our next staff meeting, I shared all the definitions I had come up with for "Humble." The goal, I explained, was to reduce this list of twenty statements down to three using a method called "Keep/Combine/Kill." As a group, we had to decide which statements we liked, which ones were duplicates we could combine and which ones we could remove from the list. It took the entire hour, but by the end, we had turned my long-winded definitions into memorable mantras. We did the same with "Hunger" and "People Smart" in the following weeks. The result was a set of co-created prescriptive principles that my team could use to make good choices in practically any scenario.

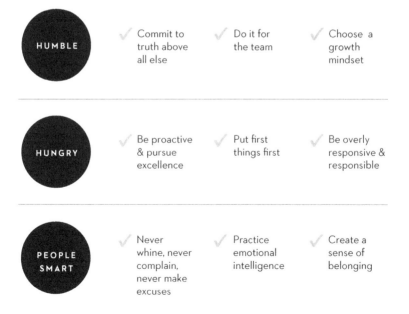

HUMBLE	✓ Commit to truth above all else	✓ Do it for the team	✓ Choose a growth mindset
HUNGRY	✓ Be proactive & pursue excellence	✓ Put first things first	✓ Be overly responsive & responsible
PEOPLE SMART	✓ Never whine, never complain, never make excuses	✓ Practice emotional intelligence	✓ Create a sense of belonging

Throughout this process, I was encouraged by the way everyone on the team weighed in and expressed strong opinions. This kind of passionate, collaborative debate would have never happened at CFNE a year ago. While engaging in it, my team showed flashes of group flow—they were completely absorbed in the task, everyone was open and listening to the others, and each person's idea built on those just contributed by their colleagues. This suggested that our shared identity was successfully creating the kind of team trust that allows people to engage in healthy conflict. Our principles meetings illustrated why this is important: healthy conflict leads to stronger commitment. When people air their opinions in the course of passionate and open debate, they are more likely to buy in and commit to the final decision. This is the crux of a leadership tactic known as "co-creating"—when people make it with you, they are more invested in it. This was certainly the case when my team helped me develop CFNE's principles, and it was enormously helpful for what came next.

HOW TO LEAD WITH PRINCIPLES

I was proud of what our team created, but I knew that was just the first step. Developing a set of principles is not leadership. **Leadership is about *operationalizing* the behaviors codified by your principles; that is, getting people to consistently use them to stack good decisions.** Not only will this result in less work for you, it will produce better results. Decisions made on principles are almost always better than ones made on a blind strict adherence to a policy.

Lead by Example

One of the ways leaders go about this is by demonstrating through our actions that our principles are important to the organization. At CFNE, for example, "embrace feedback" is a principle we talk about constantly. My staff is probably tired of hearing me talk about the importance of "entering the danger," our shorthand for difficult but necessary conversations. We shouldn't be merely *receptive* to this kind of feedback, I tell them; we should be actively seeking it out. At this point, I don't need to remind my team that the more feedback we get, the faster we improve. They know. Knowing, however, is not the same thing as believing. Knowing makes them receptive to hearing tough feedback. Belief is what they need to go *looking* for it. To help them believe, I dedicated an entire staff meeting to sharing the most powerful real-world example of entering the danger I have ever encountered. On an episode of Adam Grant's podcast, *WorkLife*, Ray Dalio describes the culture of "radical transparency" at his financial firm, Bridgewater Associates.[19] The episode starts by describing the normal response to feedback:

---

19 Grant, WorkLife with Adam. Transcript of "How to Love Criticism." https://www.ted.com/talks/worklife_with_adam_grant_how_to_love_criticism/transcript.

03:29   AG: Think about what happens when you get criticized. Like, physically: your shoulders tighten, your breath gets shallower. Negative feedback sets off alarm bells. It actually touches a nerve in your body. And psychologically? Your mind races. You start to put up shields and mount a counterattack. If you were a peacock, you'd strut. If you were an ape, you'd beat your chest. But humans have another kind of reaction. There was a study a few decades ago that said our ego can get so defensive in these situations that it becomes its own little totalitarian regime. It starts to control the flow of information to our brains the way a dictator controls the media. Think about that. Your own ego is censoring what you hear. But if we never hear criticism, we'll never improve. What would it be like in a place where people constantly criticize each other—and crave that kind of feedback for themselves in order to make everyone better? I've worked with hundreds of organizations and I found only one where that's truly the norm.

At this point, I pause the podcast to underscore the big idea I want my staff to think about: *What would it be like in a place where people constantly give feedback to each other; where people don't just avoid criticism, they crave it for themselves in order to make everyone better?* "Think about what that would be like here at CFNE," I say. "Imagine how much faster we would all get better. Imagine what this place would look like one year from now if that's how we operated." I let that thought hang in the air for a moment, then hit play again.

08:36   AG: Today, about two thousand people work there [Bridge-water Associates] and every single one of them is expected to put criticism out in the open. Even if the billionaire founder is the target. Here's an email Ray got one day from a colleague named Jim Haskel. "Ray, you deserve a 'D-minus' for your performance today. You rambled for fifty minutes. It was obvious to all of us that you did not prepare at all. Today was really bad. We can't let this happen again." When Jim sent his scathing review, Ray decided to get a few more opinions. He asked his colleagues to rate his performance that day on a scale from A to F. Then he shared the feedback with everyone else. And let me tell you, Ray did not get any As for that meeting.

09:21   RD: I sucked!

09:22   AG: I think a lot of people in that situation would have just sorted the conversation out with Jim. And you replied and you said, "Hey, everybody else in the company, I'm looping you in."

10:19   RD: I want Jim's critiques. Because I might be inclined to ramble, and because I might be inclined to not be prepared. So I made a promise to Jim: I'd do better the next time. He said, "Listen, I can't trust you to do that. And I say, "Great, I can't trust me to do that, either." And so as a regular protocol, he'll call me up, because he understands that it works well for both of us and works well for the company.

10:48   RD: It's particularly important for me to be showing anybody what I'm doing, including my failures, my successes. Yes. Why would you not do that?

11:06   RD: If your objective is to be as good as you can possibly be, then you're going to want that.

Here, I pause the episode again. I paraphrase Dalio's last line, slowly, for emphasis: *If your objective is to be as good as you can possibly be, you're going to want negative feedback.* That's it, I tell my team. Feedback isn't something to be feared or to take personally. It's a *gift* that makes us better. I underscore how criticism at Bridgewater is a two-way street where even the CEO of the firm is fair play. "I need constructive criticism as much as anyone," I tell them. "I'm depending on you guys to enter the danger with me when I screw up because the objective is to make CFNE as good as it can possibly be." Whether or not they believed this and bought into it would be determined by how I received feedback when it came. **The most powerful way leaders can operationalize their principles is to lead by example.** Remember, your team is looking to you every second for information about how trustworthy you are. Belief is trust, and it's earned when our words consistently match our actions. As the saying goes, "Your actions speak so loudly, I can't hear what you're saying."

My first opportunity to demonstrate this came a month or so later, in May 2017. After being confined to the gym all winter, many of our members were enjoying the warmer weather by hitting extra fitness outside before or after class, either in the driveway or on the side patio. A group of guys I work out with every morning during the 6:30 a.m. class had taken to doing their own workouts completely outside of class a few times a week. I would often join them, eager as anyone to enjoy the sun. After a few weeks of this, Harry approached me after the 6:30 a.m. class and asked if I had a few minutes to talk. Of course, I said, expecting a standard conversation about gym operations. Instead, Harry told me that he had noticed I had begun skipping class a few times a week in favor of outdoor sessions with the boys. "It doesn't seem fair to ask our coaching staff to take class every day when they see you doing your own thing outside of class a few times a week," he said. He was right, of course. I was embarrassed that I had given myself permission to be held to a standard lower than the one to which I held my coaching staff. I thanked Harry for his candor and committed to rejoining the 6:30 a.m. class. That could have easily been the end of that—none of the other coaches heard our conversation—but it was a perfect opportunity to celebrate something I wanted to see more of. During our next staff meeting, I recounted my conversation with Harry to the entire team and held it up as an example of how "entering the danger" makes the team better. "Great job, Harry," I said, noting that it would have been easier for him to not say anything to me at all. Harry's decision to have the uncomfortable conversation was an act of humility, I said, one that perfectly illustrated one of our principles: "Do it for the team." "That's exactly what we need to make CFNE as good as it can possibly be," I said.

By sharing that story with my staff, I also hoped to demonstrate how committed I was to our "choose a growth mindset" principle.

Praising Harry for calling me out was a signal to the rest of the team: *Ben's words are consistent with his actions. It's safe to approach him with feedback; he doesn't take it personally. The goal isn't to look good, it's to become better.* Leading by example is the most powerful tool leaders have when it comes to building trust and operationalizing the principles that will drive our organizations forward.

Teach and Tie

That said, the people on our teams are human. Of course they're not going to *always* get it right, no matter how great our principles are or how consistently we embody them as leaders. Operationalizing our principles, therefore, requires us to *coach* our teams on how to use them. I do this using a method I call "teach and tie." The idea is to proactively teach your team how to make decisions by tying them back to a specific principle. Done well, you don't just teach people how to handle one particular scenario; you teach them how to handle many potential variations of that scenario.

Over the years, I've discovered that one of the most effective ways to teach and tie is to package the lesson up as a story. Stories are a powerful way to influence behavior because the human brain is hardwired to respond to them.[20] When we hear straight

---

20 "Company, country, connections: Counterfactual origins increase organizational commitment, patriotism and social investment," Psychological Science. September 3, 2010.

facts, two areas of our brains light up: language processing and language comprehension. But when we listen to stories, neural activity increases fivefold—we're using our motor cortices and our emotion and visual image-processing centers. More of our brains are at work, so we're more focused on the story and more likely to retain it later.[21] When you package teaching moments as a story, your team can connect with the message on a personal, emotional level that will make them more likely to buy into your ideas and modify their actions accordingly.

There's an unlimited number of ways to use stories to teach. Sometimes, it's by literally telling a story. I do this often at CFNE. One of my favorite principle-coaching stories is a parable called "The Younger Brother" that perfectly illustrates one of CFNE's hunger principles. In the story, a farmer has become old and is ready to pass his farm down to one of his two sons. He sits his sons down and tells them that the farm will go to the younger son. The older son is furious. "Why would you give the farm to my brother?" he fumes. "I'm the older son, it should go to me." The father sits for a minute, thinking. "Okay," he says after a while. To the older son, he says, "I need you to do something for me. We need more cows. Will you go to Cibi's farm and see if he has

---

21 Lazauskas, Joe, and Shane Snow. The Storytelling Edge: How to Transform Your Business, Stop Screaming into the Void, and Make People Love You. Wiley, 2018.

any cows for sale?" Two days later the older son reports, "Father, Cibi has six cows for sale." The father thanks the older son for his work. He then turns to the younger son and says, "I need you to do something for me. We need more cows. Will you go to Cibi's farm and see if he has any cows for sale?" The younger son does as he's asked. Later that same afternoon, he returns and reports, "Father, Cibi has six cows for sale. Each cow will cost $200 each. If we are thinking about buying more than six cows, Cibi is willing to reduce the price to $100 per cow. Cibi also said they are getting special jersey cows next week if we aren't in a hurry, so it may be good to wait. However, if we need the cows urgently, Cibi said he could deliver the cows tomorrow." The father thanks the younger son for his work. He then turns to the older son and says, "That's why your younger brother is getting the farm."

Whenever I read "The Younger Brother" parable to my team during one of our meetings, I make a point of tying the story to our hunger principle of "Be overly responsive and responsible." Being overly responsive, I tell them, is what separates the best teammates from just okay ones. In every organization, there are a select few people who would be difficult to replace. Some people are like the older son in the story: passive and reactive. This is not us, I say. We are the younger brother. Successful people *initiate*. They are *proactive*. To illustrate why this is so important to our team's success—to teach and tie—I tell them the story about how CompTrain went from a fun side project I did for free to a multimillion-dollar company. "It started with Harry being proactive," I say. "I didn't tell Harry to monetize CompTrain. He saw the demand for it and told me he wanted to try it. It was my company, but Harry built the website, set up the payment platform and started writing and publishing the programming all on his own." By being proactive, I explain, Harry single-handedly laid the foundation for the company that CompTrain is today. Acting like the younger brother is *absolutely essential* to our team's success. Over the years, the parable has had such an impact on the team, we eventually incorporated it into our employee handbook. To this day, you can reference "The Younger Brother" to any CFNE coach and they'll instantly know what you mean.

If you're constantly looking for stories, you can find them just about anywhere. In 2017, I found one while scrolling through Instagram. One of our newer coaches had posted about her experience as a new coach at CFNE. It struck me as a cool example of our humility principles in action, so I read it aloud during our next staff meeting:

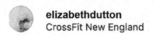 **elizabethdutton**
CrossFit New England

FOLLOW ···

A few days before I started coaching at @cfne, @harrypalley gave me my class schedule. 5:30am and 6:30am, everyday. Oh, and also... @benbergeron takes the 6:30am class everyday. No pressure.

Ben had a lot of feedback for me after my first day. And the day after that. I always knew feedback was imminent because I'd be demoing a movement or coaching a progression and Ben would put his barbell down and walk over to a window and start scrawling notes with a dry erase marker. For the first few months, this completely unnerved me. Oh god, what am I fucking up now? I'd think, often losing my train of thought or turning really red (usually both). It felt like a test that I kept failing. No matter how much I prepared, Ben always wrote on the windows. When I tightened up my cueing, he'd talk about my teach:move ratio. When I nailed the workout brief, he picked apart my general warmup.

I wrote down every piece of feedback Ben gave me, then thought through how to incorporate it into my lesson plan for the next day. It was extremely uncomfortable. Until it wasn't. After 6 months or so, I was used to it. I got comfortable being uncomfortable. And it occurred to me how much I had improved as a result—I learned more in 6 months than I had in the previous 2 years.

It was around this point that I realized something important about criticism and adversity and growth. The point wasn't to never make mistakes—what would I learn from that? This wasn't a pass/fail situation. "Winning" was not about coaching a perfect class, it was about becoming a better coach than I was yesterday. Difficult and uncomfortable were good things. They were the only things making me better.

I'm not new anymore, but I still ask Ben for feedback after almost every class. I'd be lying if I said I don't get pumped when he doesn't have any and says "great class." That's a good day. But it's a great day when he has a long list on the windows, because I get to get better.

When I finished reading this story, I made a point to teach and tie by connecting Elizabeth's acquired enthusiasm for feedback to the humility principle of "choose a growth mindset." By literally celebrating her mistakes, I hoped to signal to the team that it was safe for them to similarly stretch themselves and occasionally come up short. Mistakes are important, I told the group. They're the only way we can iterate and improve.

Stories, of course, need not be written down. Stories are everywhere. One of the most powerful ways we reinforce principles at CFNE is through oral mini-stories we call "callouts." Callouts were a new practice I initiated during 2017. I asked my staff to be on the lookout for particularly exemplary displays of our principles in action throughout the week so that they could share them during our Tuesday staff meeting. The idea was to catch each other in the act of doing great things—known as "bar-setting behaviors" in business literature. By asking my team to identify and share them, I hoped to translate abstract principles into concrete actions, decisions and behaviors. The first time we opened a meeting with callouts, I read an email I received from one of our members about something they witnessed Morgan, one of our full-time coaches, doing at the gym over the weekend:

New Message   — ⌐ ✕

From   CJ Craig

To   Ben Bergeron

Hi Ben,

I wanted to tell you about what I saw this morning at the 10:00 class. Aaron didn't have a partner for the workout and ended up shadowing a group of two other guys. I think that became overwhelming because Aaron ended up just biking on his own two minutes into the workout. Morgan, who had just finished working out at the 9:00 class, and who was totally sweaty, went to talk to Aaron and convinced Aaron to partner up with him. So Morgan worked out twice and cheered Aaron on with everything he had. He made Aaron feel important and included. He is such an outstanding person and just the type of man I want my sons to grow up to be. Just wanted you to know.

Enjoy the weekend!

A 🖉 ☺ 🖼

There are some people who can instantly make us feel important, who can light up a room just by walking in. Morgan has always been one of those people—the CFNE coaching staff used to joke that if he was a dog, he'd be a golden retriever. CJ's email described Morgan's people smarts using every principle we had—he demonstrated extraordinary emotional intelligence and he created such a powerful sense of belonging, people were writing me letters about it. The best part of the letter, however, was something it didn't say—that all of this took place on a Saturday, Morgan's day off. He wasn't on the clock. Strictly speaking, it wasn't Morgan's problem that Aaron didn't have a partner. If he had simply shrugged and left Aaron to his own devices, no one would have ever known. But that's not the kind of guy Morgan is. By sharing stories like this every week, I hoped that my staff would notice more of them and begin to mentally connect behaviors with principles. By celebrating them, I also hoped my coaches would be more likely to recognize and act on opportunities to make great choices in their day-to-day lives.

Eventually, my team understood the function of callouts and didn't rely on me to provide them. This was good, because the coaches spent more time in the gym than I did and were able to witness far more than I could. Soon, meetings were highlighting all kinds of examples of our principles that I would have otherwise never known about. For example, one of our part-time coaches, Tori Dyson, gave Harry a callout after observing him help a drop-in (CrossFit's word for an athlete visiting from another gym) who had misplaced his credit card. As she jogged on the AssaultRunner during training, Tori watched Harry—the second-highest-ranking CFNE employee—dig through the trash for ten minutes on the off chance the credit card had been accidently thrown away (it hadn't). The most remarkable thing about this was that Harry was bending over backwards to help someone who *wasn't even a member*. The guy was visiting CFNE from out of town; after today, he might never return. But if he did visit again—thanks to Harry—it would be with a sense of visiting friends. It was the ultimate example of "Create a sense of belonging." I loved that Tori caught it and recognized it for what it was. Celebrating these kinds of mostly unnoticed moments made us all more willing to go above and beyond in similarly unrecognized moments. Callouts became a virtuous cycle that incentivized excellent decisions, and CFNE's culture grew stronger with each one.

Another good way to use stories to translate abstract principles into concrete actions is through the use of "if/then" exercises. In computer programming, if/then statements are used to trigger a set of instructions. Parents use them all the time to help their kids answer their own questions: "*If* you're going to cross the street, *then* be sure to look both ways first." As leaders, we can do the same thing with our teams to help them connect principles to everyday life. During the fall of 2017, we did a series of if/then" scenarios during our staff meetings. A few days before each meeting, I sent everyone on the team a shared Google sheet with three made-up scenarios. I asked them to think about how they would handle each situation and come to the meeting prepared to discuss. For example:

CFNE IF/THEN ... SCENARIO

An athlete has gotten their name on the leaderboard for 3 of the last 4 benchmark workouts we have done. You hear rumors in the locker room that the athlete has been cheating her reps. What do you do?

I wasn't sure how aligned the team would be, but it wasn't a test. It would be a win either way. If we weren't all on the same page, the exercise and discussion would expand the team's collective-behavior template. One by one, we went around the table and shared our ideas. Below are the exact responses from my team:

CFNE IF/THEN ... SCENARIO

An athlete has gotten their name on the leaderboard for 3 of the last 4 benchmark workouts we have done. You hear rumors in the locker room that the athlete has been cheating her reps. What do you do?

Harry: Defend the individual in front of those gossiping about them. Explain that we know this individual, and if this ever did happen, it was probably by mistake. Counting is hard. Inside class, I'll watch them to see if it's an issue and, if so, cheer them on with something like "Just 3 reps to go!" to let them know I'm watching.

Elizabeth: Defend them in the locker room. Give them the benefit of the doubt. Give counting strategies generally in class while briefing the workout (chips, tallies on a whiteboard, etc), emphasizing accuracy not as it pertains to the leaderboard but in the broader context of getting fitter over time. If I notice they're legitimately shaving reps, do something during the next benchmark to make them think I'm aware of their reps—"Nice John, only 5 left!"

Morgan: I would watch the athlete in class and see if they are not doing the right amount of reps. If they aren't, assume the nobler motive. Say something like, "Why do you think you need to scale?" or "No need to stop, you only have 2 more reps left!" Assume they suck at counting and not actively shaving reps.

Tori: I would try to kill the rumors by saying that they might just have an issue with keeping track of their reps in the middle of a workout.

Dan: Thanks for bringing it up. Benefit of the doubt. I'll look into it. Observe during the next class. If it's like that I'll approach the athlete and let him/her know that he/she is strong enough or good enough to get the full ROM/rounds. Try to ingrain the right thing regardless of how hard.

To my delight, my team had very similar responses, suggesting that our principles were legitimately driving actions, decisions and behaviors. In this case, the relevant principles lived under our core value of people smart, including "create a sense of belonging" and "practice emotional intelligence." Though their answers weren't identical, my team uniformly avoided approaching the member in question in a way that might undermine their sense of belonging at CFNE or make them feel anything other than special. This, I pointed out, was amazing—it meant that we were all on the same page about the importance of trust and relationships in unlocking the potential of our clients. "You guys get it," I said. "At the end of the day, coaching is not just about seeing and correcting the members' movements. It's about connecting with our members by building trust above all else. Relationships are the secret sauce to what we're really trying to do here: improve the lives, health and happiness of our clients." Obviously, I was pleased that, for the first time in years, CFNE's principles had traction. More importantly, however, I was excited about the effect this samepageness had on my young team's confidence. Looking around the table that day, I could see the emotional bank account deposit on their faces—the calm assurance people have when they gain a sense of control over their actions and decisions. *Trust.*

•

Leading with core values is an important first step toward building culture because shared values help us get like-minded individuals on the bus. That's what I did at CFNE throughout 2016. But there's a reason the culture didn't take off right away. Without principles, my new team didn't know how to confidently handle a lot of situations they encountered. Sometimes they got it right, sometimes they got it wrong, but both outcomes were the product of doubt, uncertainty and guesswork. Teaching my team about principles helped minimize these kinds of distractions and allowed my people to direct more of their mental energy toward succeeding in their roles. This, in turn, allowed me to direct more of my own mental energy to my role as a leader. Instead of micromanaging and putting out fires, I had more time to be intentional about CFNE's organizational goals. That was good because, as retired U.S. Army General Stanley McCrystal put it, "The temptation to lead as a chess master controlling each move of the organization must give way to an approach as a gardener, enabling rather than directing. A gardening approach to leadership is anything but passive. The leader acts as an eyes-on, hands-off enabler who creates and maintains an ecosystem in which the organization operates."[22] This ecosystem is culture, the first pillar of leadership. Getting it right is the prerequisite for the second pillar: vision.

---

22 McChrystal, Stanley A., et al. Team of Teams: New Rules of Engagement for a Complex World. Portfolio/Penguin, 2015.

PART TWO

VISION

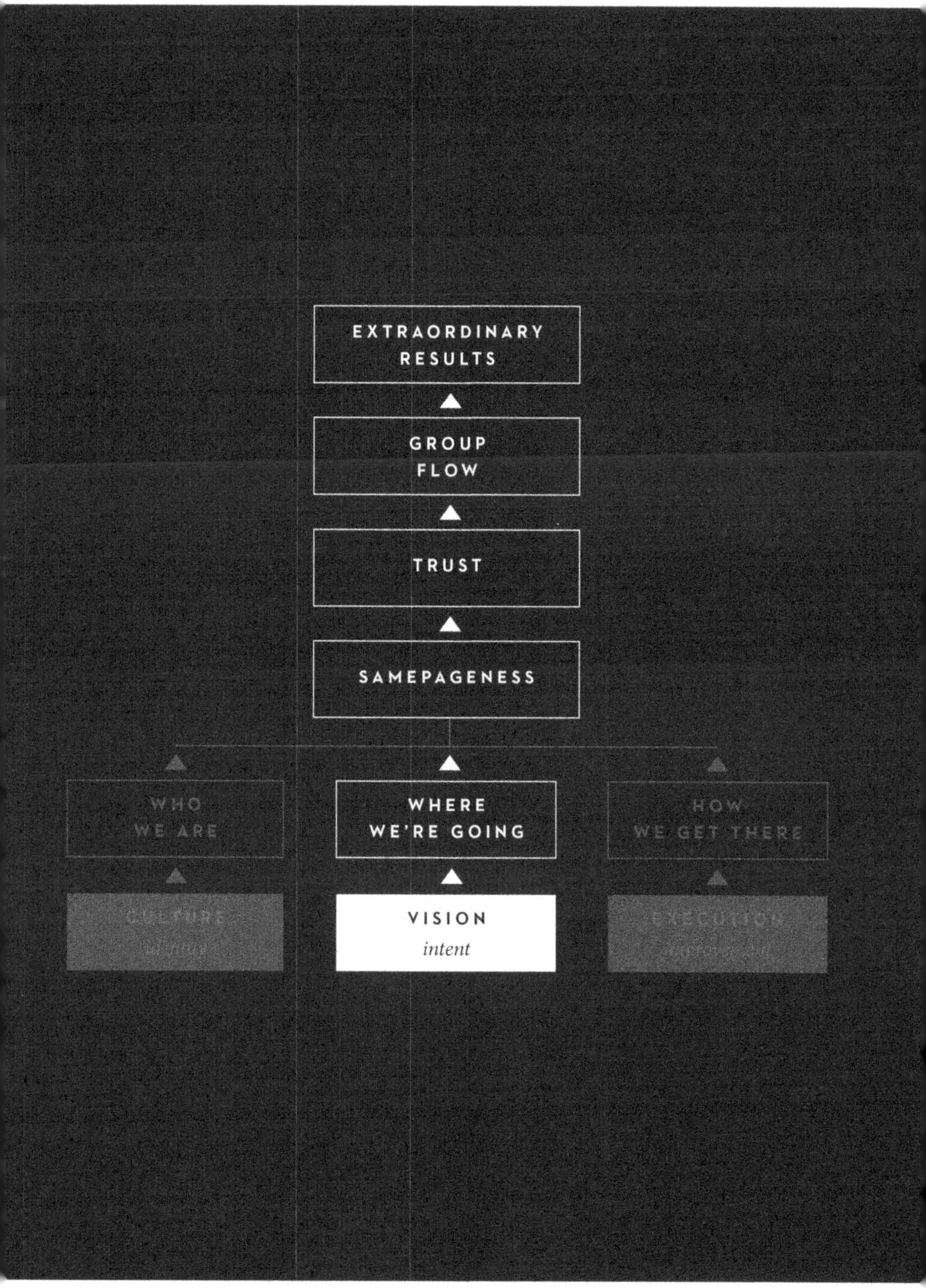
EXTRAORDINARY RESULTS
GROUP FLOW
TRUST
SAMEPAGENESS
WHO WE ARE
WHERE WE'RE GOING
HOW WE GET THERE
CULTURE
VISION
intent
EXECUTION

THE VERY ESSENCE OF LEADERSHIP IS THAT YOU HAVE TO HAVE VISION. YOU CAN'T BLOW AN UNCERTAIN TRUMPET.

Theodore M. Hesburgh

VISION

D one well, culture creates trust among our teams. The resulting samepageness is what allows people to collaborate brilliantly and tap into the performance-enhancing power of flow. But while organizations can't operate in a flow state without it, shared identity is not the only ingredient for great teamwork. To achieve group flow, our teams also need to know what it's all for. They have to understand the endgame and genuinely believe in what the organization is trying to do. **The second pillar of leadership is a direction that energizes, orients and engages our teams.** When teams don't have this kind of clarity, they underperform. When you consider what we know about group flow, this makes sense. To tap into flow, people have to be completely absorbed in the present moment and the task at hand. When people don't understand the endgame, the lack of clarity leads to apathy, which becomes a *distraction* that prevents them from being completely focused.

Once again, the solution is trust. Not in the lying vs. truth sense, but in the "I believe you prioritize my interests over your own" sense. If culture was about getting teams to trust *each other*, vision is about getting teams to trust *the organization*. Earning that trust requires leaders to be transparent about their *intentions*. Everyone on the team needs samepageness about where the organization is going and why it's going there. This, you'll recall from Chapter 1, is more or less the exact definition of "shared goals," one of the ten trust triggers that produces team flow. The strength of that trust depends on the narrative information provided by the leader. That narrative is our vision. The more clarity we create around it, the more trust our teams have in our intent.

When teams don't trust the organization, it's rarely because the leader doesn't have a vision. As leaders, we intuitively understand our vision for our organizations. The problem is we aren't adequately *sharing* that vision with our teams. This, unfortunately, is very common. An employee survey across six hundred companies by *Inc.* magazine revealed that less than 2 percent of employees can name their company's top three priorities.[23]

---

23 Coyle, Daniel. The Culture Code: The Secrets of Highly Successful Groups. Bantam Books, 2018.

In high-performance groups, it's the exact opposite—the most successful teams can rattle off their organization's vision without a second thought. This is because leaders of high-performing teams *over*-communicate their vision using narratives and signals that unite people around common shared goals. This is what we'll cover in Part 2.

In Chapter 4, we'll talk about how to get your narrative out of your head and into something tangible that you can share with your team. This clarity will allow your team to get on the same page and avoid the kind of distractions that are common barriers to flow. In Chapter 5, we'll look at the importance of relentlessly sharing (and resharing, and resharing) this vision with everyone in the organization. Doing this well, as we'll see, creates the kind of engagement that drives superior performance.

Getting our teams to trust the organization is easier if the team is composed of people who share the same values. This is why culture comes first—getting the right people on the bus makes everything easier. The ultimate goal, of course, is to actually drive the bus somewhere. Culture might be a powerful propellant, but without vision, that firepower is little more than potential. In Part 2, we'll begin converting firepower into velocity.

WE MAY HAVE ALL COME ON DIFFERENT SHIPS, BUT WE'RE IN THE SAME BOAT NOW.

———

Rev. Dr. Martin Luther King, Jr.

04

ALIGN

It's 2018 and I'm having what feels like the fifty-seventh meeting about CompTrain Gym. The topic is the same as it was in the first fifty-six meetings: Should our online affiliate programming continue to be branded as CompTrain despite its noncompetitive focus, or should it be rebranded under the CrossFit New England banner despite the fact that it serves none of CFNE's members? Harry, the head coach of both CFNE and CompTrain, is trying to explain to Patrick Cummings, our marketing director, why affiliate programming should remain a CompTrain service. Harry's calm demeanor and unfailing politeness almost disguise what I nevertheless recognize as growing frustration in his voice. I don't blame him—how many times has he made this exact point in this exact room? Patrick, too, is visibly frustrated. He closes his eyes briefly, as if trying to disarm some internal bomb. No one, however, is more frustrated than Max, the COO for both businesses. These kinds of circular, solutionless discussions offend every cell of his efficient German DNA. He's watching Harry and Patrick talk with one finger on his temple, wearing an emotion barely distinguishable from motion sickness.

In his book, *The Rise of Superman*, Steven Kotler describes the flow state as one in which every action and decision leads effortlessly, fluidly, and seamlessly to the next; a kind of high-speed problem solving.[24] I always imagine this as a buzzing hive—the kind of frenetic energy that looks chaotic but somehow isn't because everyone knows exactly what to do. Whatever is happening in this room is the exact opposite of that. If this leadership meeting had a sound, it wouldn't be buzzing, it would be cacophony—something akin to car horns during traffic gridlock. As my leadership team debates the CompTrain Gym issue, all I can think about is how this makes no sense. Harry, Patrick and Max are whip smart. They are every bit as passionate about CFNE and CompTrain as I am. They share the same values and operate along the same principles. Yet for some reason, every leadership meeting feels like a root canal. We talk in circles for hours to arrive at hard-won decisions, only to find ourselves relitigating the issues all over again the next

---

24 Kotler, Steven. The Rise of Superman: Decoding the Science of Ultimate Human Performance. 1st edition, New Harvest, 2014.

week. Lately, this has become far more worrisome to me than the fate of CompTrain Gym. My team is clearly not on the same page, and I have no idea why. Our culture, I'm almost sure, is strong. Which means that something else is blocking group flow at both CFNE and CompTrain.

THE DANGER OF MISALIGNMENT

The problem, I came to see, was that as both businesses began to grow, the divergent goals of CFNE (health and wellness for normal people) and CompTrain (performance for competitive athletes) started to confuse my team's understanding of what we were trying to achieve. I began to suspect that we all had slightly different ideas about what the endgame looked like. To Harry, CompTrain was the future and he was directing most of his energy accordingly. Patrick was more focused on CFNE, the name recognition and history of which he saw, not incorrectly, as the source of CompTrain's growing prestige. Max was somewhere else entirely; he seemed to regard the development of my personal brand—the Ben Bergeron umbrella under which both companies uneasily existed—as the logical way forward. He focused on promoting my first book, *Chasing Excellence,* building www. benbergeron.com and dramatically stepping up my domestic and international speaking schedule. This is exactly what happens when vision isn't communicated clearly: misunderstandings about exactly where an organization is trying to go. When there is a lack of clarity about a team's shared goals, people experience confusion, stress, frustration and, ultimately, failure to thrive. In 2018, this was an apt description of all my leadership meetings. It was like rowing a boat with people paddling in different directions—everyone was working hard, but frustration was high because progress was slow and exhausting. This is the cost of misalignment: inefficiency.

It's not hard to understand why it happens. As leaders, we intuitively understand our own vision, so it's easy to assume that our teams have a similar grasp of it. This, of course, is not the case. The only way your team can be on the same page about your intent is if you share it with them effectively. My problems in 2018 weren't for a lack of sharing my vision—I'm a vision guy, I talk about my vision all the time. It was that I wasn't sharing it in the *right way*. I wasn't communicating organizational intent in a way my team could understand and use to move CompTrain and CFNE forward. Apparently I'm in good company—fewer than 20 percent of leaders can distill their vision into a concrete statement.[25] The result is the kind of misalignment that existed within my business-

---

25 Craig, Nick, and Scott A. Snook. "From Purpose to Impact." Harvard Business Review, May 2014. hbr.org, https://hbr.org/2014/05/from-purpose-to-impact.

es in 2018, which was the source of the friction we experienced at practically every decision-making point. The friction is a pain in the ass, but it isn't the real danger. The real danger is that the misalignment prevents the organization from making its vision a reality. **Leading an organization that is misaligned about the vision is like driving on a road full of deep potholes—you have to drive very slowly to avoid them.**

Getting your entire team on the same page is the equivalent of paving the road. It takes a bit of time and slows things down temporarily, but once you do it you can drive as fast as you want. When everyone's on the same page, things just seem to work. Alignment is the magic that makes $1 + 1 = 3$. It's like getting star power in Super Mario Brothers—your organization gets faster and stronger and deflects everything that could potentially harm it. When your team is not on the same page, $1 + 1$ is not 2. It's more like 1.5 because the misalignment around the vision makes everything that much more difficult. When this happens, as my experience in 2018 illustrates, it's usually not a matter of team members having wildly conflicting understandings of where the business is going. It's much harder to see than that—usually a matter of just a few degrees. But those degrees matter. Even if everyone's paddling is off by just a degree or two, success becomes much more difficult to achieve.

CREATING CLARITY OF VISION

The antidote to misalignment is clarity of vision—clarity about where your organization is going, why it's going there, and how it's going to get there. There's a lot of conflicting business literature about how to create this kind of clarity, but all of it more or less encourages leaders to *summarize* their vision. Fair enough. The problem, however, is that leaders have come to believe that we have to distill the full scope of our organizational vision into a single sweeping statement—a mission statement or a vision statement or a purpose statement, depending on whom you ask. Regardless of what you call it, it's an impossible task. The result is inevitably a rambling, vague proclamation that is unmemorable and uneffective.

Clarity of vision isn't achieved in a single aspirational statement, but rather through four different elements: purpose, BHAG, mission and picture. I learned about these elements through Gino Wickman's Entrepreneurial Operating System (EOS), and have worked hard to implement them in my businesses over the years. What I've discovered is that leading an organization with just one of them is like trying to make a cookie using only flour. Yes, flour is one of the ingredients. But unless you combine the flour with the eggs, sugar and butter, you'll never have a cookie. The same is true in our organizations. To create clarity, you need to use all the ingredients of vision. Without that clarity—as I discovered while enduring fifty-seven leadership meetings about the same CompTrain Gym issue—it's impossible to execute effectively.

Purpose

The first element of vision is purpose. Purpose is the answer to the question "Why?" Why does your organization exist? If vision is about defining how your organization is going to put a dent in the universe, purpose outlines the shape of that dent. A team that truly understands and believes in a common goal can persevere through the difficult challenges inherent in any important undertaking. Purpose, in other words, serves as *intrinsic motivation*; that is, the work is so enthralling that it becomes its own reward. This is one of the hallmarks of a flow state. To access flow, we need to feel an authentic and real connection to the task at hand. Obviously, right? We're not going to put in hours and hours of focused work at the outer limits of our capacity if we don't actually care about what we're doing. This is why "shared goals" and "shared group risk" are trust triggers that lead to group flow. If the team is not working toward the same end with some skin in the game, it's much more difficult to access a flow state and unlock potential.

Of the four elements of vision, purpose seems like it *should* be the easiest one to develop, for the simple reason that our "why" almost certainly exists already. It lives inside us, as part of us. In 2018, I realized that while I understood my purpose perfectly, I had done a subpar job of sharing it with my team. The first order of business, then, was to put my purpose on paper. But it was harder than I expected. When something is that indelible to your being, you rarely give it conscious thought—it lives in your brain as a feeling, on a level deeper than speech. But since speech is a critical part of communicating purpose, developing it requires a lot of conscious thought. If you're having trouble pinning it down, I recommend using a method called the Five Whys. It's simple: Start with a descriptive statement of what your organization does—something like, "We make X products" or "We deliver X services." Then ask why that is important, and repeat five times. After a few whys, you'll find that you're getting down to the fundamental purpose of your organization. This is how I developed CompTrain's purpose statement in 2018:

CompTrain Purpose:
Transform a tribe.

The Five Whys can help leaders in any industry create greater clarity around their purpose. I recently used it to help a friend of mine who owns an audiology practice. Pat and I were talking about her business and some of the challenges that she was facing as a result of the COVID-19 pandemic. At one point, I asked her what her purpose was. She replied with the kind of generic statement that so many of us provide when asked the same question: "To provide quality care and service to our patients." I dug deeper. "Why do you do that?" I asked. Pat thought for a moment, then said, "Because that's what my practice specializes in." I smiled. "Yes, but why?" She frowned. "Because that's what I went to school for?" she replied, her tone becoming unsure. I continued to press. "Okay, but why did you do *that*?" She tilted her head thoughtfully and replied, "Because I don't think it's fair that some people have to live in a world with built-in communication barriers." I leaned forward. Now we were getting somewhere. I asked her one more time, "But *why*?" Pat threw up her hands. "Because, *Ben*," she said archly. "I think the hearing impared should be able to live the same kind of full, enriched lives everyone else does, okay?" I laughed and held my hands over my head like a referee indicating a successful field goal. "Damn," I said. "That sounds like a pretty awesome reason to go to work every day." Pat smiled back, realizing what she had done. "Yes. It is."

BHAG

One thing I did have going for me in 2018 was the second element of vision, something known in business literature as a "BHAG"—a big, hairy, audacious goal. The term comes from management consultants James Collins and Jerry Porras, who use it to describe a kind of organizational objective that will take years to achieve, if it's ever achieved at all. In some ways, a BHAG is like any other goal. It's a long-term objective informed by an organization's values and its purpose. The thing that makes a BHAG different from an ordinary goal is how ambitious it is; a good BHAG straddles the line between the possible and abject lunacy. It's the only element of CompTrain's vision that has always been clear.

CompTrain BHAG:
One million members

As Collins and Porras discovered while researching their book, *Good to Great,* a borderline-crazy BHAG is a common variable across many of the world's most successful companies. Once again, the reason is clarity. If purpose reveals the shape of the dent our organizations will put in the universe, our BHAG reveals how deep that dent will be. Purpose is a *feeling* that helps our teams enjoy their work, but a BHAG gives them something solid to work *toward.*

A good BHAG is tangible and highly focused—the kind of thing people understand right away with minimal explanation, like "climb Everest" or "make the Olympics." These kinds of goals have what I call the "Oh, shit!" effect, named for the excited response they tend to elicit when shared. To the teams charged with accomplishing them, a BHAG is more than a goal; *it's a challenge.* **This is precisely the point—great work requires a great challenge.** The irony of the "effortlessness" of flow is that it comes when teams are working their hardest, stretched to their limits in pursuit of something difficult and worthwhile. A BHAG is an important element of vision because the *challenge* of accomplishing it *engages* people in ways that unlock peak potential. Done right, it drives organizations toward significant, even unimaginable, achievement. One of the best examples is John F. Kennedy's 1962 "man on the moon" speech, in which America's president challenged the country to land a man on the moon for the first time and return him safely to Earth—arguably the most audacious BHAG in human history. The effect this challenge had on NASA was transformative. The agency's employees came together like never before to discover mathematics and invent technology that did not yet exist, so that America could do something that had never been done before. This is the surest sign of a great BHAG—when the process of achieving it completely transforms the entire organization, irrevocably, forever.

Mission

If purpose establishes the "why," and BHAG identifies the "what," the third element of vision, mission, is about the "how." **To create clarity around "how," a mission statement must answer three**

specific questions: What do you do? Who do you do it for? How do you do it differently from everyone else? For years, I led my businesses without clear, specific answers to any of these questions. As a result, everyone on my leadership team came to their own slightly different conclusions. CompTrain's poorly conceived mission created a never-ending series of distractions that prevented our entire team from tapping into a flow state.

The result, I can tell you from personal experience, feels a bit like driving on Rainbow Road, the hardest course in Nintendo's MarioKart video game. Rainbow Road is incredibly long and full of wild curves and elevation changes, challenges that are further enhanced by the road itself, which is a disorienting shade of fluorescent rainbow. But the thing that makes Rainbow Road so insufferable is that unlike every other course in the game, it is completely devoid of guardrails. When you fall off the edge, you're forced to endure an excruciating delay while your cart is extracted from the abyss and placed back on the road. Given how often this happens, the winner tends to be the player who falls off the least. Watching these people is incredibly frustrating. Their screen looks just as crazy as yours, but they somehow manage to stay on the road. It's almost like they have invisible guardrails.

In many ways, Rainbow Road is a metaphor for leading an organization. To be a successful leader, invisible guardrails are exactly what we need. In a distracting world of iridescent rainbows, mission statements provide *focus* and prevent our teams from repeatedly falling off the edge. Steve Jobs said as much in 1997 during the Worldwide Developers Conference held annually by Apple. "People think being focused means saying yes to a thing you have to focus on," he said. "But that's not what it means at all. It means saying no to the hundred other good ideas that are out there. You have to pick carefully. I'm actually as proud of the things we haven't done as the things we've done." There is great wisdom in that. Statistics show that when companies fail to thrive, it is more often due to indigestion than starvation; that is, in trying to do everything, they will eventually struggle to do anything.[26]

This is because, as Jobs suggests, the most dangerous forces trying to pull you off course are not bad luck or misfortune. The would-be saboteurs of your organization come most often in the form of *opportunities*. Some opportunities, obviously, will advance your mission. Others, however, will have the opposite effect—they are *distractions* that will dilute your mission, slow your progress or burn your organization from the inside. This is what was going on with my businesses in 2018. It's a scenario that plays out every day all over the world: A company's early success presents it with new opportunities to increase revenue and grow the brand. The reflex

---

26   Collins, James C. Good to Great: Why Some Companies Make the Leap—and Others Don't. 1st ed, HarperBusiness, 2001.

is to capitalize on these opportunities, which, after all, might not come around again. It's a thought process I'm intimately familiar with: *"Hey, we can do that! We can do that well! It'll increase our revenue! Let's go!"* This is exactly how CompTrain ended up hosting the East Coast Championship, a lucrative and high-profile event that was nevertheless completely unrelated to what we were actually trying to do. For years, the ECC drained company resources away from our mission of delivering the optimal training experience. The CompTrain coaches and staff that helped me organize the event spent at least a quarter of the year completely consumed with ECC preparations, limiting their availability to perform their usual functions within the business. Inevitably, things fell through the cracks. In the weeks before the event, those cracks became canyons. The needs of the ECC prevented us from serving the needs of CompTrain's subscribers in the ways they had come to expect. It was a broken promise not only to our customers but to my staff, whose focus was constantly being shifted and redirected towards new initiatives with no obvious connection to our purpose.

It's not hard to see why this kind of EBA withdrawal prevents teams from operating in a group flow state—people won't put their heart and soul into something if they expect to be working on something entirely different in a month or two. The guardrails of a well-crafted mission statement create consistency, allowing people to pour their hearts into their work. When I decided to cancel the

ECC, it was for all of these reasons, despite the fact that the event was over 20 percent of yearly revenue at the time.

A good mission statement gives you the kind of invisible guardrails you need to ensure that every action you take, no matter how big or small, keeps you *focused* and moving straight ahead. How? It's simple—every time you're faced with a decision, consider each choice through the prism of your organization's mission. Is this in line with what your organization does, who it does it for, and what makes it different? These are the questions I began asking myself toward the end of 2018, for both CompTrain and CFNE.

CompTrain Mission:
Create the optimal training program for competitive athletes by combining and innovating with the best practices of group and individual training.

Your mission should help you find the path and *stay on the path* by giving you a framework to discern which opportunities are power and which ones are poison. When you analyze your choices against your organization's mission, the right decisions have a way of making themselves.

Picture

By now, you may have picked up on a pattern within the four elements of vision. Each one provides an added layer of specificity—

purpose outlined the big "why," BHAG took it a bit further and defined "what" and mission drilled down a bit more to identify "how." This pattern of specificity implies an important point about "shared goals"—everyone in the group working towards the same end—as they pertain to group flow. In order for teams to collaborate seamlessly, they need a high level of samepageness about what those goals are exactly. Achieving group flow is more likely when teams can draw a boundary, however temporary or virtual, between the activity and everything else.

This is the function of the fourth and final element of vision. "Picture," as Gino Wickman calls it, drills down with even more specificity to outline what your organization will look like inside and out in three to five short years. It takes the form of fifteen to thirty bullet points that, together, illustrate the not-so-distant future. By taking the time to imagine the future you want to create, the gaps between that future and where you are now reveal where you should be focusing your efforts. Think of it like a dot-to-dot image from a children's coloring book—what starts out as a shapeless collection of dots becomes, as they're connected, an actual *picture.*

To create CompTrain's picture, I asked the members of my leadership team to think about what the business would look like in three to five years if it was making progress toward our BHAG of getting one million people onto our platform. I asked everyone to come up with ten to fifteen bullet points and to come prepared to discuss them. I began the meeting by combining everyone's bullets into one master list. Our goal, I said, was to use the Keep/Combine/ Kill method to reduce it to fifteen to thirty items. The result, for both CompTrain and CFNE, was a kind of organizational to-do list.

CompTrain Picture:

Organizational
- Twenty thousand paid subscribers
- One million free users
- Small, streamlined team of ten to twelve full-time employees
- All weekly leadership meetings ranked at nine or higher
- No one works more than sixty hours/week

Product/Coaching
- A.I.-driven personalized programs for users
- Five in-house Top 20 CrossFit Games athletes
- Two assistant coaches for Ben
- Four CompTrain Camps per year
- One to three CompTrain Gym Open Houses per year
- Building additions for dedicated CompTrain gym/training space
- Expanded office space with private conference rooms
- "12 Classes Strong" at CFNE
- Fully built-out and implemented customer journey for CFNE

Marketing
- Hire three-plus customer experience coaches
- Weekly Live chats with CompTrain coaches
- Churn rate less than 4 percent
- Sponsor and impressive presence at Semifinal competitions
- One Annual affiliate gathering paired with a Semifinal competition

IT
- Release second version of CompTrain App (CT2.0)

The goal isn't necessarily to hit your exact three-year picture, but to create samepageness about where your organization is going. Unlike purpose, BHAG and mission, "picture" can and should be subject to change as market dynamics shift. At CompTrain, this is a rolling process that we repeat every year. Creating this kind of detailed picture allows my leadership team to begin charting a path forward by working backwards from a future we can all vividly imagine.

●

With all four elements of vision in place, the CompTrain Gym issue that plagued our leadership meetings for much of 2018 practically resolved itself. Understanding the company's big end goal of one million people on the platform helped us assess whether or not our CompTrain Gym product—a business-to-business (B2B) offering for coaches, not athletes—had a place in a business-to-consumer (B2C) company whose target market was competitive athletes. Far from being a distracting outlier in the product lineup, we realized that our affiliate programming was an important part of our go-to-market strategy, as individuals following CompTrain Gym programming at an affiliate were much more likely to know about and take advantage of the various individual product offerings. By taking the time to articulate and operationalize the four elements vision, my team was able to not only understand how CompTrain

Gym fit into the equation, but to begin leveraging it as a means to further the company's overarching vision.

It would be wonderful if clarity were the default state of teams. Unfortunately, telepathy doesn't exist yet, so instead the default state of teams is misalignment and confusion. Over time—as strategies shift, plans change and teams grow—things tend to become even more confusing. Moving teams from confusion to clarity is one of the most vital functions of leadership. To help you do this within your own organization, I've included the vision document we use at CompTrain, as well as a blank template you can use to think about the four elements of your own vision. My hope is that by taking the time to fill it in, you will save yourself the wasted time, energy and frustration that come from leading an organization without the level of clarity these elements provide around your "how," "what" and "why."

As you begin to use it, keep in mind that articulating vision is not a set-it-and-forget-it task. Just because your team is aligned behind the vision today doesn't mean they will *stay* aligned. The work to maintain that clarity continues indefinitely—maintaining alignment is just as much a part of our jobs as creating it. The only way leaders can do this is by reviewing and discussing the vision with our teams often. Every team meeting, every important document, every project kickoff, every onboarding session is an opportunity to repeat the four elements and explain how the work at hand connects to the organization's vision. Clarity will never be perfect, but the more of it you can create among your team, the more samepageness you'll have and the faster your vision can become a reality.

PURPOSE

Purpose is the answer to the question "Why?" Why does your organization exist?

CompTrain Purpose:
Transform a tribe.

BHAG

A wildly ambitious long-term goal that is guided by your organization's values and purpose.

CompTrain BHAG:
1 million+ members

MISSION

A wildly ambitious long-term goal that is guided by your organization's values and purpose.

CompTrain Mission:
Create the optimal training program for competitive athletes by combining and innovating with the best practices of group and individual training.

PICTURE

A picture of what your organization will look like on the inside and out in three to five years.

CompTrain Picture:

- Twenty thousand paid subscribers
- All weekly leadership meetings ranked at nine or higher
- No one works more than sixty hours/week
- A.I.-driven personalized programs for users
- Five in-house Top 20 CrossFit Games athletes
- Two assistant coaches for Ben
- Four CompTrain Camps per year
- One to three CompTrain Gym Open Houses per year
- Building additions for dedicated CompTrain gym/training space
- Expanded office space with private conference rooms
- "12 Classes Strong" at CFNE
- Fully built-out and implemented customer journey for CFNE
- Hire three-plus customer experience coaches
- Weekly Live chats with CompTrain coaches
- Churn rate less than 4 percent
- Sponsor and impressive presence at Semifinal competitions
- One Annual affiliate gathering paired with a Semifinal competition
- Release second version of CompTrain App (CT2.0)

PURPOSE

Purpose is the answer to the question "Why?" Why does your organization exist?
To pull it out, use the "Five Whys" method: Start with a descriptive statement like,
"We make X products" or "We deliver X services." Then ask why that is important five times.

BHAG

A wildly ambitious long-term goal that is guided by your
organization's values and purpose.

MISSION

Mission statements consist of three elements. They should define:
What You Do + Who You Do it For + How You Do it Differently Than Anyone Else

What You Do:

Who You Do It For:

Your Competitive Advantage:

PICTURE

A picture of what your organization will look like on the inside and out in three to five
years. It takes the form of fifteen to thirty bullet points that, together, illustrate what
your organization will look like in the not-so-distant future.

-
-
-
-
-
-
-
-
-
-

-
-
-
-
-
-
-
-
-
-

IF YOU WANT TO BUILD
A SHIP, DON'T DRUM UP
PEOPLE TOGETHER TO
COLLECT WOOD AND
DON'T ASSIGN THEM TASKS
AND WORK, BUT RATHER
TEACH THEM TO LONG FOR
THE ENDLESS IMMENSITY
OF THE SEA.

Antoine de Saint-Exupery

05

ENGAGE

By 2019, CompTrain had begun to resemble the business it is today. The defining feature of the company's evolution was a switch from a reactive, make-it-up-as-we-go organizational modus operandi to a more intentional, forward-looking approach. Nothing was more illustrative of this shift than the addition of an annual CompTrain staff retreat, the first of which was held in September. We rented a beautiful house in Newport, Rhode Island—a two-hour drive from Boston—for the occasion. My main goal was to simply allow my young team to spend some quality time together, but I also built in a few short work sessions to plan the company's direction for the coming year.

On the first day, after completing a somewhat overprogrammed team workout of running and burpees, we break out into groups. Harry and Dan, who oversee the product side of the business, go downstairs to talk programming while Elizabeth, Allan, Julian and I huddle upstairs to talk marketing.

I begin this first session by bringing Beth, who has been CompTrain's media lead for the last four years, up to speed about a structural change Allan and Julian are already aware of: Effective immediately, Allan will be leading CompTrain's new *marketing* team, and Beth will report to him. I can practically feel her bristle at the news. The expression on her face is thunderous. This is not surprising—Beth is good at many things, but hiding her feelings is not one of them. More to the point, she has been running this department more or less by herself since 2016. Practically anyone would interpret this kind of change as demotion, but that's not what it is at all. "This isn't a reflection of your performance in any way," I reassure her. "The company has just grown into a place where we need to be more deliberate about marketing, not just media. Creating content is only one part of marketing, and that part isn't going to change. You'll continue to do what you have always done so well, and Allan will handle some new elements, like market research and using data to develop strategy." I save the final selling point for last. "You won't have to come to the weekly leadership meeting anymore," I say, referencing the ninety-minute meeting of department heads that takes place each Thursday. "The only real change here is that you're going to have *more* time to spend on the things you enjoy doing and that move the needle for the company." Beth seems to see the logic in this because her body language relaxes somewhat. At least, she no longer looks like a volcano on the verge of erupting. I congratulate myself for narrowly avoiding an emotional bank account withdrawal and our newly restructured marketing team goes on to have a productive week of planning. Everyone on the team returns to Boston invigorated and eager to put new ideas in motion.

In the weeks that follow, however, something about Beth seems to change. She starts coming into the office later and leaving earlier. She is more reserved around her teammates and less opinionated in meetings. The creative energy that always made her so good at her job seems dimmer, and she looks increasingly to Allan to assign her projects. The quality of her work, which had been exemplary for four years, loses some of its panache. And, more worryingly, she isn't the only one. Within CFNE too, some of my most historically engaged employees are showing similar signs of flagging commitment. This makes no sense. Prior to the fall of 2019, people like Beth, Morgan and Dan were among the *most* engaged people on the team. By now, I know enough about leadership to understand that there are no bad employees, only bad leaders. Something I'm doing—or not doing—is undermining commitment at both CFNE and CompTrain.

THE DANGER OF DISENGAGEMENT

When people are committed, everything they do is infused with purpose, energy and enthusiasm—they understand their role, they know how their role contributes to the success of the organization and they want to do the work. In leadership parlance, this is known as engagement. When leaders share their vision well, engagement is the result. When they don't, as I learned the hard way, the opposite occurs—disengagement. In Beth's case, the shift could be traced back to the changes that were made to CompTrain's leadership team during the staff retreat. Prior to Newport, Beth had attended CompTrain leadership meetings in her capacity as the team's media lead; after Newport, Allan took her place at those meetings as the team's marketing lead. Once I recognized it, a pattern emerged. Within both CFNE and CompTrain, all the most committed members of the team were part of the leadership team, and all the less engaged people were not.

The more I thought about this, the more obvious it became. The people who made up the CFNE and CompTrain leadership teams attended weekly meetings in which the vision was discussed and debated in detail, which gave them insight into the organization's *intent*. Their access to me, their roles as managers and their knowledge of the vision gave people like Harry and Allan a clear-eyed understanding of the big picture. They understood the vision that the business was working toward, and the prospect of achieving it excited them and made them feel more invested in their jobs. The rest of the team, who did not attend leadership meetings and therefore had far less insight and understanding of the overall vision, did not. To them, the future was much more *uncertain*. In Chapter 1, we learned why this is problematic. **People will not—biologically cannot—reach their full potential when they're facing uncertainty.** When the pattern-seeking human brain lacks sufficient information to make sense of the world, it is ruled by stress. When leaders communicate the vision clearly and effectively, we decrease the cognitive load on our teams and allow them to be present, focused and energized. Sound familiar? It should—these are the hallmarks of a flow state. And that's precisely why individual engagement is so important—because it is a critical element of group flow. As Vince Lombardi once explained: "Individual commitment to a group effort—that is what makes a team work, a company work, a society work, a civilization work." As I discovered in 2019, getting your vision out of your head and on paper is only half the battle. The much bigger task is *sharing* that vision with your team—your *entire* team—in a way that unites them, excites them and galvanizes them into action.

As leaders, we are the only ones who can do this. Only the leader is in a position to see how all the elements of vision fit together, which means that we are the only ones who have enough perspective to communicate it, reinforce it and help people recognize when they may be drifting from it. Doing this well is a full-time job, but research suggests that many leaders are not doing it at all: Only 29 percent of employees can correctly match their company to its publicly espoused strategy. The result is that people aren't engaged at work, to the tune of 69 percent—a full *two-thirds of our teams*—according to Gallup.[27] If you're trying to unlock the potential of your organization, it goes without saying that you can't do it with one-third of your team. **Extraordinary achievement requires extraordinary engagement—of *everyone* on the team.** Indeed, research shows that highly engaged organizations and teams massively outperform those with any amount of disengagement.[28] This is because engaged employees behave differently. Engaged team members are more productive, more proactive and better problem-solvers. They produce better results, need less oversight and take more accountability for their performance. To unlock the potential of organizations, leaders need to generate this kind of engagement among every individual on the team.

27   Devinney, Timothy. "Corporate Social Responsibility and Corporate Governance: Comparative Perspectives." Corporate Governance: An International Review, V21, No 5, 413-419. www.academia.edu, https://www.academia.edu/3745889/Corporate_Social_Responsibility_and_Corporate_Governance_Comparative_Perspectives.

28   Inc, Gallup. Gallup Q12® Meta-Analysis. Gallup.Com, https://www.gallup.com/workplace/321725/gallup-q12-meta-analysis-report.aspx.

HOW TO ENGAGE YOUR TEAM

The only visions that take hold are *shared* visions. Leadership, therefore, includes getting our teams to see our vision as their own. Engagement occurs when people feel that they are making a contribution to something or someone they value. There is a parable I like that illustrates why this is so powerful: A traveler comes upon three bricklayers building a church. He asks the first man what he is doing. The man replies, "I'm laying bricks." The traveler asks the second man the same question. "I'm putting up a wall," he says. Then the traveler repeats the question to the third man, who smiles and says, "I'm building a house for God." Think about that for a second. All three men are doing the same thing, but their perspectives could not be more different. Only the third man understands not only what the vision is, but what it *means*. He's not just putting up a wall. He's building something important—sacred, even. Skill level being equal, which bricklayer would you hire? The smart money is on the third man, who is clearly the most engaged in the work.

As leaders, it's on us to give the people on our teams a similar sense of meaning. In a world where over two-thirds of people are disengaged at work, we can dramatically improve what our organizations are capable of by simply sharing our vision with our people. This kind of transparency allows every individual in your organization to feel like they are a part of something bigger. It's the scene from "Miracle," when the players realize they are representing the United States of America, not their alma mater. It's no surprise that that's when the 1980 U.S. Olympic hockey team started clicking. **Engagement is what happens when everyone on the team plays for the name on the front of the jersey, not the one on the back.** This was the mistake I made when I removed Elizabeth from CompTrain's leadership team during the Newport retreat. So much of her engagement, I realized too late, came from the sense of meaning she derived by being so connected to the vision for so long. By suddenly severing that connection, I inadvertently undermined a key source of her engagement and, as a result, her performance.

To correct this problem at CFNE and CompTrain, I experimented with dozens of different ways to ensure that my entire team—not just those in leadership positions—knew and understood the vision. I created a shared vision document, hung posters in the gym offices and handed out quarterly booklets outlining our current goals and how they supported the broader CFNE or CompTrain objectives. Such methods are useful, but none, I've discovered, is as effective as the "teach and tie" method—the same narrative technique I used to get my core values and principles to stick in Part 1. It is as true of vision as it is of culture: **To engage our teams, leaders must be storytellers, explaining our vision through a never-ending series of stories.** Our job is to take the vision off the page and craft a narrative that helps every person on our team build bridges between the present and a meaningful future. When it comes to vision, these narratives should be centered around explaining 1) organizational decisions, 2) organizational changes and 3) organizational results. To teach and tie, we must seize all three as teaching opportunities and tie them back to one of the four elements of vision.

Decisions

To remedy CFNE's and CompTrain's flagging engagement in 2018, I began using the four elements of vision as a segue into practically every conversation, starting with the easiest low-hanging fruit: explaining decisions. As leaders, it is in our best interest to keep our teams in the loop about decisions, big or small, regarding the organization. This goes beyond transparency, which, while good, often amounts to little more than public service announcements. To help our people connect to our vision and see it as their own, we have to explain *why* a decision was made *through the context of the vision*. It was the latter, I realized, that I failed to do when explaining the changes to the CompTrain marketing team to Elizabeth in Newport. I had explained the decision and why it was being made, but I hadn't tied the why to the broader organizational vision. When this dawned on me a few weeks later, I sat down with her to fill in the gaps.

This, it must be said, is what I should have done from the beginning. I cringe when I think about the way I broke the news to Elizabeth during the 2019 CompTrain retreat—during a strategy meeting, in front of a group of her peers, with the bedside manner of Genghis Khan. This is the exact opposite of how changes should be announced; nobody should ever be surprised in a group setting, ever. Not only did I make Beth feel demoted, I forced her to endure the insult of that perceived demotion in front of her co-workers. I didn't give her any time to process the change. She wasn't able to ask any questions about it. Everything about the way I handled that situation suggested to Elizabeth that she did not belong; that she wasn't safe. Her relatively stoic reaction in the moment camouflaged the full extent of the damage I did to our relationship that day. In a span of a single five-minute conversation, I significantly undercut five years' worth of trust. In the months after, I gained a new appreciation for an oft-quoted maxim: "Trust takes years to build, seconds to break and forever to repair."

Having the one-on-one conversation I should have had with Elizabeth before the CompTrain retreat seemed like a good place to start. "Our goal is to launch CompTrain to the moon," I explain to Beth. "We have one hundred thousand members right now, but we're trying to grow that community to *one million*. The content you've created over the last few years has gotten us into a position where that is now achievable. But it will be no small task to grow *ten times* our size in the coming years. I've been meeting with people in other industries that have scaled up like this, and everyone agrees that marketing is the rocket fuel. We need to start doing things like market segmentation analysis, A/B testing, data-driven marketing campaigns, SEO optimization and technical analysis of every aspect of the user experience." I pause for a moment to gauge Beth's reaction. She wrinkles her nose, as if smelling something unpleasant. "That makes sense," she says. "But none of that is in my wheelhouse." I agree, but tell her she's earned the right to be as involved as she wants to be. "Are you interested in making these aspects of marketing part of your wheelhouse?" I ask. Beth shrugs. "Not really," she admits. "I'm a creator. I like making things." I nod. I expected as much. "Cool. Then let's keep you focused on content," I say. "We're spending so much of our leadership meetings on the technical side of marketing, to the point where they are now probably a distraction from your role as a content creator—and we need your amazing content if we are going to continue to grow to a community of one million." When I finish, Beth is nodding in animated agreement. Understanding not just *why* the decision was made but *what* that decision is intended to achieve—our BHAG of one million CompTrain subscribers, in this case—has completely changed how she feels about it. "I'm good at social media, but I'm not that good," she jokes, acknowledging that nine hundred thousand new subscribers is well beyond the scope of Instagram alone.

As we talk, I am struck by the speed at which this line-of-sight diffuses all Elizabeth's concerns: Knowing the big-picture goal makes the decision feel logical instead of personal. Almost instantly, she sees the new marketing efforts as supporting her role instead of threatening it. Add it to the list of mistakes I made in Newport: teaching without tying. The following graphic illustrates the continuum for explaining leadership decisions. Number two represents how I originally explained the changes to Beth's role at CompTrain and shows just how far off the mark I was.

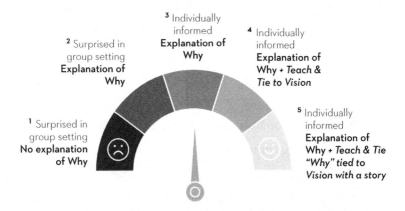

Obviously, simply laying down the law is easier and faster. But when leaders take the time to tie the decision back to one of the four elements of vision, we provide everyone on our team with what is known as "line of sight" between their day-to-day tasks and the broader goals of the organization. Line of sight is where real engagement starts. It helps the individuals on our teams contextualize their efforts, which allows them to feel a sense of ownership in the endgame. And when people feel ownership over their work, they are more committed to it by a factor of five to one.[29] No wonder "shared risk" is one of the ten trust triggers that leads to more flow—having some skin in the game is a powerful intrinsic motivator.

To create line of sight, we have to talk about our vision *constantly*. Explaining decisions in the context of the vision is an important (and frequent) opportunity to do this. This can often seem like overkill to us as leaders. But understand that we live with our vision twenty-four hours a day, seven days a week, 365 days a year. We know every nuance of it and how it all fits together. Our teams do not. What seems like overkill to us is the bare minimum for them, as I learned all too well in Newport. My task going forward was to create line of sight for everyone, not just the people in leadership positions.

Change

Another important opportunity to teach and tie is during periods of change. As a general rule, people hate change. Our brain inter-

---

29   Keller, Scott. "Increase Your Team's Motivation Five-Fold." Harvard Business Review, Apr. 2012. hbr.org, https://hbr.org/2012/04/increase-your-teams-motivation.

prets change as a threat and responds by releasing fight-or-flight hormones. We feel a loss of control, confusion and uncertainty. We are hardwired to resist change because change makes us feel unsafe. Yet bringing any vision to life by definition requires change. As leaders, we have to overcome our team's psychological barriers to change. As ever, the solution is trust. We can cushion the blow of change by contextualizing it in terms of how it will positively affect the future, then explain how it represents a concrete step toward making that future a reality.

I navigated this at CFNE when we decided to introduce a new system for members to register for classes. In the past, all CFNE classes were open to all members, with no sign-up required. However, the popularity of a few class times meant that some classes often had thirty or more members while other class times were consistently closer to ten. The discrepancy in attendance caused issues at both ends of the spectrum; from safety and individual attention in the bigger classes to lack of excitement, engagement and competition in the smaller classes. Given this reality, a new system was needed to optimize member experience. The solution was to introduce a formal registration system—an app our members could use to sign up for specific class times. The biggest change was a twenty-four-person cap on each class—if more than twenty-four people signed up, they would be placed on a waiting list. The new system represented a significant break with past CFNE policy, and I knew it would probably be unpopular. Whether the members got on board or not would depend on how the coach of their class explained the change and answered their inevitable questions. Which meant I had to introduce the change to my staff in a way that got them excited about it.

Based on my experience with Beth, I begin not by announcing the decision to change class registration, but by giving a macro-level overview of our shared vision for CFNE. "As you guys know, our goal is to be the best gym in the world," I say, to a chorus of nodding heads. "Part of that," I continue, "is creating '12 Classes Strong,' meaning that every single CFNE class provides an optimal experience for every member." More nods—the idea of 12 Classes Strong is something my staff is familiar with because it's part of our three-year picture and we are constantly defining and refining what an "optimal experience" means during our weekly staff meetings. "We're not there right now," I say, stating the obvious. I zoom in now to the micro-level issue at hand. "Some classes regularly have thirty to thirty-five people attending, while others have only eight to ten." More nods, particularly from the coaches who have to regularly modify their lesson plans to account for an extra ten to fifteen people. Now that they understand the context, I introduce the solution—the change. "Going forward, we're going to try to get closer to 12 Classes Strong by introducing a class sign-up system." I spend the next few minutes explaining the details of the new app, the twenty-four-person caps, and the waiting list. Before I open it up for questions, I finish by zooming back out to a macro view of the CFNE vision. "12 Classes Strong is one of the most critical elements of our three-year picture," I say. "This new system is going to be a game changer for the quality of the coaching we can provide in class, which will translate to our members having more fun, getting fitter, improving their lives and helping them kick ass into their nineties." This macro-micro-macro approach is the key to effectively teaching and tying. I was pleasantly surprised at how well it worked. While some coaches had questions about the details, no one had any reservations about the system itself.

I could have easily announced the new system in five minutes and walked away from that meeting satisfied that I had honestly and transparently communicated with my team. Strictly speaking, that would have been true. But it still would have been a miss, because I wouldn't have created total alignment between our agreed-upon, understood vision and the new changes being made. Not lying is not the same thing as samepageness. By taking forty-five minutes to explain *why* the decision was being made in the context of the broader CFNE vision and taking the time to answer my staff's questions, I gave them line of sight between their day-to-day roles and our shared future. "Over-communicating" in this way created a sense of safety—trust—that allowed my team to feel individual ownership over the new policy. That engagement was invaluable in earning the support of the members when we rolled out the new system a few weeks later. Without understanding how the micro fit in with the macro, I felt sure, the change would have been wildly unpopular and required me to spend valuable time— far more than forty-five minutes—answering dozens of perturbed emails and phone calls.

Results

Ultimately, it's not enough to simply *say* that your vision will create a brighter, better future. **To sustain engagement, leaders have to prove that the vision is, in fact, having the impact that was promised.** Multiple studies have shown that when people understand the impact of their contributions, they're more likely to bring their best effort every day. A 2009 medical study, for example, found that when a digital photograph was attached to a patient's file, radiologists produced significantly more thorough reports—they were longer, included more recommendations, and contained more incidental findings.[30] In a questionnaire that was also part of the study, the radiologists said that the photos helped them relate better to the patients, whom they seldom meet face to face. Another study similarly found that restaurant cooks prepared

---

30   Kraft, Dina. "Radiologist Adds a Human Touch: Photos." The New York Times, 6 Apr. 2009. NYTimes.com, https://www.nytimes.com/2009/04/07/health/07pati.html.

higher-quality food when they could see their customers from the kitchen.[31] In both cases, performance increased when people could see the tangible impact their work had on real people. This is the final piece of the engagement puzzle: **To inspire your staff to do good work for you, you have to find a way to express the organization's impact on the lives of customers, clients, students, patients—whomever you're trying to serve.**

At CFNE, I do this by occasionally inviting members to our weekly staff meetings to share how the gym has impacted their lives beyond the gym. The point is to show the coaches, all of whom became coaches because they wanted to make people's lives better, that their impact is often much deeper and more profound than fitness gains in the gym. The stories are always powerful. One member, a Palestinian-American woman who teaches at Wellesley College, told us about how her office was once vandalized with anti-Arab sentiment, and how the psychological damage inflicted by the incident was so profound, she retreated completely from social life for over a year. The support she received from the CFNE coaches and the friends she made at the gym, she said, gave her the confidence and strength to completely turn her life around. The coaching staff listened to Nadya's story with wide, tear-filled eyes.

---

31 Editors, H. B. R. "Cooks Make Tastier Food When They Can See Their Customers." Harvard Business Review, Nov. 2014. hbr.org, https://hbr.org/2014/11/cooks-make-tastier-food-when-they-can-see-their-customers.

To them, she had always been the shy woman who had unexpectedly blossomed into the ringleader of the notoriously rowdy 6:30 a.m. class. But until that day, they had never appreciated the full depth of that transformation, or the incredibly important role they played in bringing it about. Another member, Shaun, shared how the determination, gratitude and positivity he learned from the CFNE coaches became a kind of protective armour during a traumatic adoption process in which custody of his child was granted, then revoked. He described how the CFNE mindset of "control what you can control" allowed him to endure the painful separation period and the strain it put on his family.

For coaches who value improving people's lives, these kinds of stories are important. They show that their coaching has an impact, that what they do *matters*. Being able to see that impact fills us all with a renewed sense of purpose. It inspires us to continue bringing our very best each day because we understand that our very best is making a difference.

•

For the longest time, I thought employee engagement was about getting my employees to care as much about my vision as I did. It took me years to realize the futility of this. It's just not a reasonable expectation. No matter how expertly you share your vision and show it in action, your team is never going to care about your organization as much as you do. But that doesn't mean they'll never be as *engaged* as you are. They can be, if you share your vision with them by creating narratives that tap into the shared identity we created in Part 1.

This is one of many reasons why culture must always come first. Without shared values, even the best leaders will struggle to engage their people. This may seem like common sense, but too many leaders are so focused on managing processes and attending to the formal aspects of task performance that they neglect to create the kind of shared identity that facilitates shared vision. Everything we've talked about in Part 2 is similarly foundational to what we'll talk about in the final chapters of this book: execution.

PART THREE

EXECUTION

```
┌─────────────────────┐
│    EXTRAORDINARY    │
│      RESULTS        │
└─────────────────────┘
           ▲
┌─────────────────────┐
│       GROUP         │
│       FLOW          │
└─────────────────────┘
           ▲
┌─────────────────────┐
│       TRUST         │
└─────────────────────┘
           ▲
┌─────────────────────┐
│    SAMEPAGENESS     │
└─────────────────────┘
```

WHO WE ARE	WHERE WE'RE GOING	HOW WE GET THERE
▲	▲	▲
CULTURE	VISION	EXECUTION
		improvement

THE GROWTH AND DEVELOPMENT OF PEOPLE IS THE HIGHEST CALLING OF LEADERSHIP.

———

Harvey Firestone

EXECUTION

Now that we've built a shared organizational identity and a clear vision, it is finally time to start bringing that vision to life. Execution is where the rubber meets the road. It's about building a bridge between where our organizations are now and where we want them to be in the future. Execution is the third and final pillar of leadership, but far too many leaders, myself included, make the mistake of starting here. It's easy to understand why—this is the work (or lack of work) that we can *see*. If results were a tree, execution would be everything above the ground, while culture and vision would be the roots hidden below ground. How tall a tree ultimately grows up, of course, is dictated by how deep its roots are able to grow down. To unlock the full potential of our organizations, leaders have to focus on growing the roots first. *Execution has to come last.* I get it—growing a strong culture and creating clarity of vision might not seem as urgent as the many day-to-day things that impact your organization's bottom line *right now*, but they are absolutely critical to its ability to unlock its potential down the road. Rushing the execution actually delays the results, or worse. A tree without roots, after all, is destined to become a log.

With strong roots in place, we can safely focus on execution. If culture was about getting our teams to trust each other and vision was about getting the team to trust the organization, execution is about getting everyone on the team to trust us as leaders. This is important because execution is all about improvement, and improvement is inherently uncomfortable. Our job is to develop our people into more productive versions of themselves, which requires us to do two things: Find weaknesses, then systematically attack them. This is the two-sided coin of execution, and only leaders are in a position to do it well. We are the only ones who can ask the tough questions that everyone needs to answer and use what we learn to close the gaps between where the organization is now and where it wants to go. These are two distinct skill sets, and we'll explore both in Part 3.

We'll begin in Chapter 6 by focusing on how leaders can identify the problems in their organizations. I'll share some of the strategies I've puzzled together over the years to probe for them constructively, and we'll see how the quality of the information we glean hinges on the strength of our relationships with the individuals we lead. In Chapter 7, we'll shift to the hands-on side: developing the skills of the people on our teams so that their performance, and that of the organization, continuously improves. Whether you're a military commander, a middle-school teacher or a small business owner, this kind of leadership takes the form of feedback. As we'll see, the way we deliver it matters as much as the information itself.

To unlock extraordinary performance, leaders must master both sides of the execution coin. Like most of the lessons in this book, I learned this one the hard way: You cannot solve problems you cannot see, but seeing problems is not the same thing as solving them. Until we can do both effectively, our execution will be incomplete and ineffective. And without the ability to execute, everything we've worked so hard to build up to this point—culture and vision—becomes hollow. In the end, success is never about the idea; it's always about the execution. Author Adam Grant makes this point in his book, *Originals*: "If we want to forecast whether the originators of a novel idea will make it successful, we need to look beyond the enthusiasm they express about their *ideas* and focus on the enthusiasm for execution they reveal through their *actions*."

FOR THE STRENGTH
OF THE PACK IS
THE WOLF, AND
THE STRENGTH OF THE
WOLF IS THE PACK.

Rudyard Kipling

06

EXPOSE

After a decade of two steps forward, one step back, CFNE was, by the end of 2019, finally on solid ground. With a strong culture and clarity of vision, the gym was running better than it ever had, and with far less effort on my part. For the first time, I felt like I actually knew what I was doing. It felt like beating a video game—having defeated all the threats and removed all the barriers, I could now roam freely through all the realms. So that's exactly what I did: I left.

Okay, I didn't leave, exactly. But I did begin to dedicate more of my time to other business ventures outside of CFNE—namely CompTrain, which had recently eclipsed the gym as the organizational breadwinner. Since the two companies share a building, I was hardly abandoning CFNE. I simply began delegating more of its day-to-day management to my leadership team. I also stopped coaching my 8:30 a.m. class and attending weekly staff meetings. I was confident that, having reached a kind of business maturity, the gym would mostly run itself. And for almost a year, it did. As far as I knew, CFNE was running smoothly and everyone was thriving in their roles.

In January of 2020, I learn otherwise.

I'm having a meeting with Micha Thaddeus, my talented new gym manager, to debrief her first week. Micha, however, has something else on her mind. "I've noticed a few things this week," she begins, in the manner of a doctor preparing to deliver bad news to a patient. "Ben, the entire staff is overworked, burned out and frustrated." The problem, she says, is that almost nothing is functioning as intended; the discrepancies between vision and execution are not gaps so much as yawning chasms. "Take the new elements program, for example," Micha says, with a glance down at her notes. "The private-school model that you've created and implemented looks good on paper but is, in practice, a nightmare for the coaches tasked with overseeing it. New members love the personalized workout emails they receive every night throughout their first month, but composing these emails has effectively chained Morgan to his computer." Forget about advancing the vision, Micha says grimly—CFNE is barely treading water. In some areas, we are actually sliding backwards. The lively content that Elizabeth once created as the gym's media manager, for example, has all but dried up as CompTrain—which pays the other half of her salary—demands a disproportionate amount of her attention. The front-desk position, meanwhile, is a revolving door of temporary employees that the gym struggles to replace. Front-desk shifts that can't be covered are apparently being piled onto already overstretched coaches or simply not being covered at all. As Micha rattles off problem after problem, I realize just how removed I have become from CFNE over the last year: *I am completely out of touch.*

I wasn't sure what was worse, the fact that the gym was chock full of problems I had failed to notice, or that none of my employees had thought to bring them to my attention. *Why wouldn't they just ask me for help?* I thought. The idea that my team didn't feel like they could talk to me wounded me personally, but it also worried me. Was the lack of trust symptomatic of deeper cultural problems? Unlikely, I decided. It wasn't that my team was afraid to ask for my help—it was that they were *unable* to ask for my help. For the last year, I hadn't been around enough for anyone to ask me much of anything. With the possible exception of Elizabeth, who coached the 6:30 a.m. class I attended most days, I could not remember the last time I exchanged more than pleasantries with Morgan, Dan or Tori. For the last year, I had not been leading CFNE—I had been presiding over it.

WHAT IS EXECUTION?

It's not a coincidence that when I stepped away from CFNE, the gym's execution started coming off the rails. The problem was that I, like so many leaders, regarded execution as something I could delegate so as to have more time to focus on "bigger" issues. This notion, as I discovered, is completely wrong. To understand why, we have to first understand what execution means. Most leaders think of execution as doing all the things that will get an organization from Point A to Point B. Strictly speaking, this is not untrue. In practice, however, execution is about *solving* all the *problems* that *prevent* an organization from getting from Point A to Point B. Here's the rub: Solving problems is hard, even when we know exactly what they are. If we don't know what the problems are, we stand no chance at all. Executing, therefore, is as much about identifying problems as it is about solving them. As Ray Dalio said, "Truth—more precisely, an accurate understanding of reality—is the essential foundation for producing good outcomes." **Execution starts with identifying the gaps between the way things are supposed to work and the way they actually work in practice. It's about exposing reality.** Leaders who execute well are masters of sleuthing out every barrier and inefficiency preventing their organization from reaching its goals and bringing its vision to life. Think of this as organizational intelligence. As leaders, our job is to gather as much of it as we can.

I learned the hard way that this is impossible to do if you're anything other than deeply engaged in your organization's execution. If you think about execution as coaching, it seems painfully obvious: How good would a sports team be if the coach spent all his time in his office scheming up strategy while delegating all of the actual coaching to an assistant? The most effective coaches constantly observe their teams on the field and in the locker room. That's how coaches get to know their players, learn their capabilities and understand how they interact with one another. It's no different for leaders in any other organization. When teams struggle to execute, it is almost always because the leader is, as I was throughout 2019, too disconnected from the action. The resulting blow to the organization is twofold: We cannot see the problems undermining our organization's execution and the people on our teams cannot bring them to our attention.

HOW TO FIND PROBLEMS

To close CFNE's execution gaps in 2020, I needed to fix both problems. To get the business back on track, I had to figure out where it was coming off the rails—but I couldn't do it by myself. I needed my team to show me, then work with me to come up with viable solutions. Simply being in the gym more wasn't going to do the trick. I needed to systematically, not passively, expose reality at every level—to identify gaps between the way things should be done and the way they were actually getting done.[32] What I discovered is that there is not a one-size-fits-all solution. To uncover problems, leaders have to probe for them in a variety of different and complementary ways. In the first part of 2020, I had the most success with three: 1) managing by walking around, 2) being a customer of my own product and 3) conducting energy audits. Think of each one like a slice of swiss cheese. One slice is full of holes, but if you stack a few slices together, the holes overlap to the point where there are no more holes.

Manage by Walking Around

If the goal is to expose reality, the best place to look for it is in its natural habitat: on the front lines. It is very difficult to identify organizational problems from behind a conference table or over email. No amount of technology can beat the value of face-to-face interaction. To understand the problems facing the organization, leaders have to get out to see people on their turf.[33] This is the first thing I started doing after my meeting with Micha. I began spending a lot more time at CFNE. Most of this time was unstructured; I

---

32 Bossidy, Larry, et al. Execution: The Discipline of Getting Things Done. Revised edition, Crown Business, 2009.

33 Abrashoff, D. Michael. It's Your Ship: Management Techniques from the Best Damn Ship in the Navy. Warner Books, 2002.

didn't want to have meetings about what was going on (or not going on). I wanted to witness it. I took the pulse of the place by simply wandering around the gym and asking questions of my coaching staff. In business circles, this is known as "MBWA"—managing by walking around. The benefit of MBWA is that by randomly sampling events and employee discussions, leaders are more likely to identify and facilitate improvements to morale, sense of organizational purpose, productivity and total quality management of the organization, as compared to sitting in the office and getting information secondhand from a handful of managers.

The main benefit of managing by walking around, however, is that it makes it easier for the people on our team to express themselves and their ideas. People are more comfortable in their own environment. Conversations with superiors feel more organic there; they are more casual, less threatening. As Marine Corps General Jim Mattis said, "Troops will tell you things when they're on guard duty in the dark." As a battalion commander preparing his troops for the Persian Gulf War, Mattis made a habit of walking the lines at night, hopping into fighting holes to chat with shivering sentries. In his book, *Call Sign Chaos*, he describes spending as much time as he could with his "grunts," assessing their hopes, anxieties and frustrations, as well as their readiness for the coming war. In doing so, Mattis demonstrated a keen grasp of the art of managing by walking around. The goal is not to just meet with people. The goal is to feel what our people are feeling and put ourselves in their shoes. By connecting with our people on their turf, we can gain their perspective and leverage it to improve the entire organization. The following exchange illustrates how Mattis—then a lieutenant colonel—went about it in Afghanistan:[34]

> **General Mattis:** "How's it going, lads?"
> **Marine:** "Oorah! Fine, sir, terrific. Living the dream ..."
> **General Mattis:** "We both know that's bullshit. We're stuck in the middle of nowhere while we want to be killing Al-Qaeda. Level with me. Give me something I can fix."

Mattis's approach is the opposite of a well-worn leadership slogan: "Don't bring me problems; bring me solutions." Research by organizational psychologists shows that leaders who focus too heavily on solutions inadvertently encourage a culture of groupthink. To make sure that problems get raised, leaders need mechanisms for encouraging people to challenge the status quo. Asking our people to give us a problem we can fix is a valuable way to both expose reality and enhance our personal relationships with those we lead. As I wandered around CFNE in early 2020, howev-

---

34 Mattis, James N., and Francis J. West. Call Sign Chaos: Learning to Lead. First edition, Random House, 2019.

er, I encountered unexpected resistance—it was difficult to get my coaches to speak candidly. My troops didn't talk to me like General Mattis's talked to him. When I asked Bud Henry, the newest member of the coaching staff, to give me a problem I could fix, he was visibly reticent. He smiled his 50-megawatt Bud smile and insisted that whatever he might be struggling with was his problem, not the gym's. "I'm still figuring this whole marriage thing out," he said, with a self-deprecating laugh. "I just need to get better at time management." When I told Micha about this later, she gave me a somewhat pained smile, like a parent patiently trying to explain something to a child. "Of course he said that," she said, noting Bud had initially given her the same response. It was only after a lot of probing that she got to the heart of the matter. "Every single one of the coaches would rather die than say something to you that might make you think they aren't humble, hungry or people smart," she explained. "That's why they're all suffering in silence. They don't want to be branded as complainers." I gaped at her. Surely my team understood the difference between complaining and giving candid feedback. (Complaining is talking about a problem. Feedback is talking about a problem with a solution-oriented mindset.) With an arch of her eyebrows, Micha issued an unspoken challenge. *"Do they, though?"*

This raises an important point about MWBA. Even the right questions can fail to identify problems. What counts is the substance of the communication and the nature of the person doing the communicating. In performance cultures, an emphasis on results often undermines psychological safety. When we see people get punished for failures and mistakes, we become worried about proving our competence and protecting our careers. We learn to engage in self-limiting behavior, biting our tongues rather than voicing questions and concerns. Sometimes that's due to power distance: we're afraid of challenging the big boss at the top. That's what was happening at CFNE in January 2020. My conversations at CFNE were producing next to no substance. My employees, who apparently interpreted my questions as some kind of core values test, were giving careful, calculated answers. U.S. Army General Colin Powell said that the day soldiers stop bringing you their problems is the day you have stopped leading them: "They have either lost confidence that you can help or concluded you do not care. Either case is a failure of leadership." One month after my initial conversation with Micha, this was about the only thing that *was* clear to me. My staff's hesitation to speak candidly suggested the gym's problems were much bigger than the elements on-boarding process or the front desk schedule.

That problem—and what General Powell was describing—is a breakdown of trust. Trust, as we saw in Chapter 1, can be broken in any number of ways. In my case, trust was undermined by the distance I had inadvertently put between myself and my staff throughout much of 2019. That distance had created a communication barrier between me and the people on the front lines. I had assumed—wrongly—that the strong personal relationships I had developed with the people on my team gave me license to be less involved in the organization. But relationships aren't coins we can collect and put on a shelf. Relationships are more like plants—they require constant nurturing or they die. In distancing myself from my team, I unintentionally signaled that my relationship with them was not important. Of course they didn't seek me out to bring problems to my attention—they thought I didn't care.

It's not hard to understand why this is problematic, right? Leaders don't work on the front lines, so our ability to execute depends on the candid perspective of the people who do. Execution occurs at the speed of trust—when it breaks down, so does our intel.[35] Managing by walking around requires healthy levels of trust—trust I no longer had. In order to identify problems, I was going to have to earn it back. Since relationships are the wellspring of trust, that's where I started—nurturing my personal relationships with the people I led. The stronger those relationships became, the more candid our conversations became, and the more our execution improved.

---

35 Covey, Stephen M. R., and Rebecca R. Merrill. The Speed of Trust: The One Thing That Changes Everything. 1st Free Press trade pbk. ed, Free Press, 2008.

If something as soft as relationships strikes you as too opaque to affect something as firm as execution, consider the disaster of Space Shuttle Columbia. In 2003, Columbia exploded during re-entry into the Earth's atmosphere, killing all seven crew members on board. In its report about the causes of the accident, the Columbia Accident Investigation Board concluded that while the explosion was ostensibly caused by an errant piece of foam, the underlying issue was a disconnect between NASA engineers—the people on the front lines with the first-hand information—and Columbia mission leaders responsible for using that information to make decisions. Investigators found that NASA's engineers had a strong sense that the Columbia might have been severely damaged during liftoff, but did not voice their concerns because NASA management was not open to hearing them. In some cases, the report says, undesirable information was overlooked or dropped from briefings.[36] After the Columbia launch, for example, an engineer asked for clearer photographs to inspect the damage to the wing, but managers didn't supply them. In a critical meeting to evaluate the condition of the shuttle after takeoff, the engineer didn't speak up. What doomed Columbia was not a lack of technology or ability, but a lack of *leadership*. **Relationships are critical to effective leadership.** When

---

36 Columbia Accident Investigation Board. National Aeronautics and Space Administration, Aug. 2003.

NASA failed to appreciate just how critical, seven people died and America's thirty-year space shuttle program was permanently shut down. An extreme example, no doubt, but one that illustrates the extent to which a leader's personal relationships affect the entire organization's execution.

Let me clarify: I am not an advocate of being best friends with the people you lead. Being too friendly can jeopardize your authority and undermine your leadership. The trap of wanting to be liked is an easy one for all leaders to fall into—I fell into it myself in CFNE's early days. It took me years to realize that my team needed a leader, not a buddy. The irony is that our people like us more when we focus less on being liked and more on offering guidance and support. It's a tricky but important needle to thread. As General Mattis said, we must consistently maintain a certain social and personal distance, remembering that there is a line we must not cross. But we should come as close to that line as possible without surrendering one ounce of our authority. When we pull this off, the result is strong relationships with the people on the front lines of our organizations, people on whom we can depend for candid insights. Doing this well is time consuming and takes significant personal effort but, as Stephen Covey reminds us, we cannot be *efficient* with people—we can only be *effective*.

Being effective, from a leadership standpoint, means addressing the problems we encounter. If execution occurs at the speed of trust, solving problems is one of the most effective ways leaders can speed it up. In the early part of 2020, this was a critical part of reconnecting with my staff and rebuilding the trust I lost in the past year by being asleep at the switch, so to speak. After talking with Morgan about his eighty-hour work week, for example, we worked together to make elements on-boarding more sustainable for the coaches implementing it. The personalized nightly emails to new members sounded great in theory, but their impact on attendance was wholly disproportionate to the work required to send them, so I scrapped them. CFNE's social media problems were a similar case of good-on-paper but bad-in-practice. Assigning Elizabeth to lead both CFNE and CompTrain media sounded efficient in theory, but the complete opposite goals of the two organizations—long-term health vs. competitive success—meant that, far from repurposing content for both brands, she was essentially doing two full-time jobs. To remedy this, I decided to pull Beth out of CFNE altogether and make her a full-time CompTrain employee. This move allowed us to bring a part-time CFNE coach, Tori Dyson, on staff full time to manage CFNE's social media. This kind of action demonstrates that we are listening to our people and deepens their trust in us. In keeping with George Washington's approach to leadership, we must listen, learn and help—then lead.

Be a Customer of Your Own Product

If you lead a business, another surefire way to expose reality in your organization is to experience that reality firsthand. If you own a business, become a customer of your own product. I've made a lot of execution mistakes over the years, but I have always been consistent on this point—I have been attending CFNE's 6:30 a.m. class for the better part of a decade. It's not the most efficient use of my time, but taking class every day allows me to experience the gym's product the same way our clients experience it: I go to the same website to check the workout each night. I sign up for class using the same system our paying members use. I go through the same warm-ups they do, use the same equipment, follow the same programming, receive the same coaching and use the same app to record my scores. Over the years, doing this has exposed all manner of execution glitches: coaches rushing through warm-ups, the CFNE app not updating, typos on workout descriptions and bugs in the sign-up process. If I'm having trouble signing up for class, the vast majority of our members are probably running into the same issue. Solving these problems improves the member experience, but it would be impossible to do without being a customer of my own product.

The same principle applies regardless of what kind of organization you lead. If you own a restaurant, dine there with your friends and family. You might think your service is top notch, only to discover that the food comes out cold. If you own a navigation app, use it whenever you drive around town. You might think your crowdsourcing function is excellent, only to discover untapped avenues to increase its accuracy or ease of input. If you own a shoe company, order your products online the same way everyone else does. You might be satisfied with the quality of your gear, only to discover that shipping is too slow. No matter what kind of business you're in, becoming a customer of your own product is an important way to expose deviations between desired and actual outcomes. Great leaders use this process to constantly raise the bar, improving quality throughout the organization.

Energy Audit

As leaders, we are the only ones who understand the complete vision—not only what it is supposed to look like in practice, but what it's supposed to *feel* like in practice. When we manage by walking around, we can gain a sense of the former. But the latter—the "vibe," as I like to call it—is much more difficult to assess than the tangible aspects of execution. But vibe is just as important. To understand why, think of a hostess welcoming people into a restaurant. It's the hostess's responsibility to greet the customers, ask them how many people are in their party and escort the group to an appropriate table. If she does these things, the hostess is doing her job and the front of the restaurant is executing well, right? Not necessarily. If the goal is extraordinary results, following a procedure to the letter is the price of admission. How effective the hostess is comes down to how she makes patrons *feel*. As a guest's first point of contact with the restaurant, she sets the tone for their entire experience. Does she smile warmly and make eye contact? Does her tone and speaking style match the atmosphere the restaurant is trying to project? Does she pick up on subtle social cues of her guests and respond accordingly? A great hostess fills the room with a warm energy that positively influences the emotional state of the atmosphere. For a restaurant trying to execute at the highest possible level, getting the vibe right matters every bit as much as policies and procedures.

The trouble is that energy is not something we can see. Something as ethereal as a feeling cannot be assessed in a meeting or summarized in a report. Feelings must be felt. To get a sense of our organization's vibe, we have to do what I've come to think of as "energy audits." In a documentary about Eleven Madison Park, the best restaurant in the world in 2017, owner William Guidara describes how it's done: "You walk in, you go to the corner, you close your eyes and you just listen. You can hear it in a room when it's a good night. It's the way that the room sounds. The chatter, the energy—there's a fullness to it when you know everything is just clicking."[37]

---

37 Warren, Michael John. "7 Days Out." Eleven Madison Park, 2, Netflix, 21 Dec. 2018, https://www.netflix.com/title/80207124.

As Guidara suggests, the idea is to blend into the background of your organization—wherever the action is—and simply take it all in. Reading an atmosphere is extremely tricky, as any meteorologist can attest. And since no one has yet invented the emotional equivalent of a super Doppler radar, leaders have to do it the old-fashioned way—by observing. We are not looking for anything specific. In fact, we're not *looking* for anything at all. We're trying to gauge the atmosphere of the experience so that we can compare it to the ideal—the feeling as it exists in our vision. This requires what detectives refer to as "soft eyes"—a slightly unfocused gaze that takes in the whole field of view at once, all together. Soft eyes allow investigators to see the scene as a cohesive whole in order to fully understand it. "Hard eyes," by contrast, see nothing but the object of their focus. This was a big part of my problem in 2020—I didn't spend enough time in the gym to assess the tangible aspects of execution, let alone the intangibles.

Today, I make a point of conducting regular energy audits. In a CrossFit gym, the intangible side of coaching is known as "presence and attitude." It is the ability of a coach to create a positive, exciting and engaging learning environment. When I lean against an unassuming wall and absorb a CFNE class, I'm watching for this with soft eyes, looking at everything and nothing. I take in the collective body language, tonality, enthusiasm and interpersonal dynamics of the entire group the same way a meteorologist takes in temperature, humidity, precipitation and air pressure. All of it is data that can be used to measure the metrics that matter most to me: warmth, joy, trust and camaraderie.

When our CFNE members tell me what they most love about the gym, these are the things they describe. It rarely has anything to do with fitness. More than anything, our clients want to feel like they're part of something special. They want to feel welcomed and cared for, respected, inspired and motivated. The same is true of practically every organization. Atmosphere is a critically important factor in driving results. If execution is about exposing the problems in our organizations, the problems we *cannot* see or touch are every bit as important as the ones we *can* see and touch. It's important for leaders to have a system to identify both kinds. Because when it comes to execution, getting "good" results is a relatively straightforward matter of improving the tangibles. But it's improving the intangibles that unlock potential and move organizations from good to great.

•

Managing by walking around, being a customer of your own product and conducting energy audits are effective ways to expose reality, but practicing them well depends on one all-important leadership trait: humility. Everyone tends to have their own definition of humility, but my favorite is something Bob Gaylor, a retired Air Force chief Master sergeant, said. "Humility must never be confused with meekness. Humility is being open to the ideas of others." **Being open to the ideas of others is a critical part of execution.**[38] It allows us to acknowledge our mistakes. This is important because even the best leaders are bound to make a lot of mistakes. The more we can contain our egos, the more realistic we can be about the problems facing our organizations. Fortunately, by the time Micha sat me down in the beginning of 2020, I had twelve years of running my own business and had long since accepted that I did not have all the answers. I am constantly swallowing my pride and turning inward. It's funny how often the problem is you. Did I clearly articulate the goals? Did I give my people enough time, training and resources? Did I listen to their concerns? This mindset, it turns out, was just as fortunate as the timing of Micha's intervention. I had no way of knowing how critical those eight weeks were.

And then COVID-19 happened.

---

38   Wooden, John. Wooden: A lifetime of observations and reflections on and off the court. The McGraw-Hill Companies, Inc. 1997.

66

THE ONLY
SAFE SHIP
IN A STORM
IS LEADERSHIP.

—

Faye Wattleton

07

COACH

In normal circumstances, execution starts with finding problems. In 2020, problems found you. In March, the coronavirus pandemic exploded in the American Northeast. Two weeks later, gyms across the country—including CFNE—were forced to close as official shelter-in-place orders were handed down by state legislatures from Massachusetts to Florida to California. Like so many other businesses, my gym had to figure out how to survive during a national quarantine with an unknown end date. Would the shutdown last two weeks or six months? What if it lasted a year? The problems I had been contemplating in the first few weeks of the year seemed trivial compared to the ones COVID-19 dumped on us. My new Swiss-cheese strategy for problem identification was put to an immediate and brutal test—The Year of Our Lord 2020. A trial by Dumpster fire.

When we were forced to close the gym in March, I assumed the biggest problem would be figuring out how to continue delivering CFNE's service to our members without the ability to conduct physical classes the way we always had. The apparent solution was Zoom video conferencing, which allowed us to conduct virtual workouts that people could do from home. After six weeks of Zoom classes, however, I realized I had been wrong. The biggest problem wasn't figuring out how to deliver CFNE's service virtually. The biggest problem was that it was *impossible* to deliver CFNE's service virtually.

Technically, we were doing it—we published daily workouts and held coach-led Zoom classes five times a day. But CFNE's programming has never been the product. The product—the magic that changes people's lives—is our *coaching*. And every member I reached out to said the same thing: It just wasn't the same over Zoom. By the end of April, a single data point provided incontrovertible evidence of this fact: Over half of CFNE's four hundred members had cancelled their memberships. Two hundred and fifty customers, gone. We needed to find a way to stop the bleeding—and unless we did it soon, CrossFit New England would not survive the pandemic.

Actually, we needed to do more than stop the bleeding. If CFNE was going to survive, we needed to find a way to get our members *back*, and there was only one way to do that. Since coaching people in person was the secret sauce, we had to find a way to coach

CFNE classes in person again. Obviously, state law prevented us from doing this in the gym the way we always had. But CFNE had a huge parking lot, and the weather was getting warmer. What if we could somehow hold classes outside? Legally, there wasn't anything preventing us from doing this. Unfortunately, there were a lot of other things preventing it. Safely running classes outside would be a huge lift—financially, logistically, meteorologically. It was a big decision, but the Four Elements of Vision made it an easy one. If holding classes in person was the secret sauce, we had to do everything in our power to make it happen.

So we did. In May, my staff and I began assembling an outdoor gym in the CFNE parking lot. To be COVID-safe, we built individual, socially distanced workout stations. We bought a few thousand pounds of stall mats and spaced them twelve feet apart in three rows of eight, for a total of twenty-four stations. To mitigate rain and heat, we bought 10-foot-by-10-foot tents for each one and secured them with four cinderblock tethers. The next step was power—we ran extension cords from the gym to the parking lot to power the clock, lights and the stereo system. Morgan built a stand for a whiteboard so that we could display the workout and all the usual scaling options. It wasn't a perfect solution—we still had to adjust the programming around the lack of a pull-up rig— but it was a hell of a lot better than Zoom. With this setup, we could resume CFNE group classes through the fall.

Building it turned out to be the easy part. The key to making it work was developing systems and protocols to ensure that twenty-four members could safely assemble and work out together during a pandemic. We created systems for the bathrooms, systems for running workouts and systems for contact tracing in the event one of our members received a positive COVID-19 test. The biggest challenge was the equipment. When members arrived, they had to be able to get barbells and plates and kettlebells without congregating. Their equipment had to be completely sanitized when they picked it up and re-sanitized again when they brought it back. Clean and dirty equipment had to stay separated. To pull all this off, my team created socially distanced equipment staging zones—one for clean equipment and one for used equipment. Signage posted on the grounds indicated how this should flow and prevented people from gathering too closely outside their workout stations. Used equipment was washed by a staff member, who then transported it to the clean station.

Because the coaching staff was busy leading their classes, most of this labor fell to CFNE's front-desk staff—namely, John Czekanski, Matt Desalvo and Tabitha Daily. The three of them spent all day, every day cleaning barbells and bumper plates and lugging them back and forth from gym to the parking lot. Even with shorter classes designed to give them sufficient time to do this, it was a tight turnaround. Because they were always on the front lines, John, Matt and Tabitha also ended up problem-solving when things inevitably went wrong. Two weeks into parking lot classes, for example, John arrived at work at 5:00 a.m. and discovered that all twenty-four tents had been torn down by a thunderstorm. He had thirty minutes to figure out how to make the space functional for the 5:30 a.m. class, which he had to do in pre-dawn darkness. Every day, it seemed, came with some new obstacle to overcome.

Day after day, my team overcame them all. Pulling off COVID-safe group CrossFit classes in a parking lot was an extraordinary amount of extra work for all of us. Most of the time, it wasn't much fun. But it was worth it—after a few weeks of parking lot classes, CFNE had regained one hundred paying members. I knew CFNE wasn't out of the woods yet—with so many unknown variables, only time would tell if the business would survive COVID—but by finding a way to continue delivering our product, we had given the gym a fighting chance.

THE OTHER SIDE OF EXECUTION

In retrospect, it makes perfect sense that CFNE's members wanted to be coached in person. On the competitive side of Cross-Fit, top training programs had been moving away from a remote model of coaching since well before COVID. Across the country, an in-person "training camp" model was being adopted by many of the top coaches and programs, including CompTrain. There seemed to be unspoken consensus that coaching CrossFit Games athletes in person translated into faster improvement and better performance. Of course, the same would be true for regular CrossFit athletes. The same is true for everyone, everywhere. The best technique for achieving expert performance in every field—including writing, teaching, sports, programming, music, medicine, therapy, chess and business—is known as "deliberate practice." Unlike regular practice, in which we work on a skill by repeating it again and again until it becomes almost mindless, deliberate practice is a laser-focused activity. It consists of stretching yourself just outside your comfort zone, stopping and reflecting when errors occur, making adjustments and continuing this process over time. **Deliberate practice is most effective when conducted with some kind of coach who can give feedback, point out errors, suggest techniques for improvement and provide vital motivation.** Although mastering any skill requires a lot of time engaging in solitary practice, working with a coach at least some of the time is incredibly valuable. In some fields such as sports and music, it's common for a coach to be present all the time. No wonder CFNE's Zoom classes weren't effective—the virtual format made it all but impossible for the coaching staff to give their athletes the *real-time feedback* they needed to improve performance.

As leaders, we're trying to do the exact same thing within our organizations. **If the first half of execution was about identifying problems, the second half is about solving them—it's about improving the performance of our people so that our organizations can achieve the big, hairy, audacious goals we set for them.** It's about constantly improving everything we do until we close the gap between where we are now and where we want to be. In sports, this is universally recognized as coaching. If power cleans are on the menu at CFNE, for example, I demonstrate what the movement should look like, teach the athletes in my class how to do it, then relentlessly give them feedback until they can do it flawlessly. I do the same thing with my CrossFit Games athletes, and it's the best part of the job. Coaching is fun. Helping people improve their performance is gratifying. Though the task is functionally identical for leaders beyond the sports world, we have a different name for feedback in an organizational setting: accountability. Like coaching, accountability is about holding people to agreed-upon expectations by addressing the gaps between expectations and performance. Unlike coaching, most leaders do not enjoy accountability—*at all.* According to the *Harvard Business Review,* accountability is the number-one most-shirked leadership function.[39] No matter how

---

39 Kaiser, Darren Overfield and Rob. "One Out of Every Two Managers Is Terrible at Accountability." Harvard Business Review, Nov. 2012. hbr.org, https://hbr.org/2012/11/one-out-of-every-two-managers-is-terrible-at-accountability.

tough a game we may talk about performance, when it comes to holding people's feet to the fire, many leaders tend to step back.

In 2020, I was one of them. At the same time I was bending over backwards to return CFNE's brand of coaching feedback to our members during a global pandemic, I completely stopped delivering that kind of feedback to my employees. The new work-from-home setup, virtual Zoom meetings and the looming existential business crisis were barriers that made a hard thing harder. It was easier to not give my staff feedback during COVID, so I didn't. The irony was rich: Here I was, moving heaven and earth to give my athletes access to CFNE's magical feedback, while completely neglecting the source of that magic. My mistake is illustrative of a phenomenon that predates COVID-19. **For some reason, the kind of feedback that coaches give on a playing field becomes extremely uncomfortable when given practically anywhere else. On a playing field, people are receptive to feedback. In an office, it totally freaks them out.** This might be because many leaders don't think of it as feedback; they think of it as *criticism*. Criticism is uncomfortable and unfun, so we avoid it like the plague. You can see how this will eventually become problematic—the second half of execution is about improving performance by solving problems, but it's impossible to solve problems or improve performance without the kind of feedback we negatively associate with accountability.

Fortunately, there's a simple solution. **To execute at the peak of our potential, leaders have to flip how we think about account- ability.** A paradigm shift is all that stands between us and the kind of execution we need to transform our organizations: **Leaders are not prison wardens; we're** *coaches*. The fact is there is nothing inherently negative about giving feedback—for all practical pur- poses, it's the same thing as coaching. If we approach accountabil- ity like coaching, we can dramatically improve what our people, teams and organizations are capable of.

THE ART OF COACHING

To be good coaches, leaders need to do two things: The first, ob- viously, is to give technically sound feedback—our ability to im- prove performance will never exceed our technical expertise. Sound feedback, however, is not necessarily the same thing as *effective* feedback. To be effective, feedback has to actually create change. **The most successful coaches—and the best leaders—not only give expert feedback, they deliver it in a way that inspires people to** *act on it.* **Which is why, when it comes to feedback, delivery matters as much as substance.**

For Type A leaders who make a religion out of results-orient- ed objectivity, this can be a tough pill to swallow: If we're masters of our craft, why should delivery matter at all? If the information we're delivering is accurate, why is the packaging important? Because we're not leading robots; we're leading *human beings*. We know from Chapter 1 that the human brain processes information through an emotional filter that is highly evolved to detect danger. If we deliver feedback in a way that makes our people feel attacked or threatened or ostracized, they're unlikely to hear a word we say.[40] This evolutionary biology is why the delivery of feedback matters—humans can only perform to their full potential when they feel safe and secure. **Improving performance requires trust. Sound feedback is essential, but trust is what makes it effective.** This is what sets CFNE's coaching—and the results of its members—apart. Athletes who trust their coach will do just about anything the coach asks of them.

This is what gives in-person coaching an edge over virtual classes. It's not that our members are coached in person so much as what that in-person coaching creates: Trust. My eight-thirty members' absolute trust in me, developed through years of working together every day, makes them receptive to my feedback. When they implement it, they do so with enthusiasm and to the absolute best of their ability. In a fitness model based on *high intensity*, this is everything. Relationships enhance the quality of our members' practice, which enhances their performance.

---

40 Carnegie, Dale. How to Win Friends and Influence People. Pocket Books, 1936.

In that sense, the real challenge for leaders isn't just getting our people in a position to get real-time feedback—it's getting them to actually *hear it.*

HOW TO DELIVER FEEDBACK

As leaders, we face the exact same challenge. We have to learn how to deliver feedback in a way that creates the kind of trust people need to act on it. Overriding the brain's highly sensitive fight-or-flight response is like trying to get past the three-headed dog guarding the Sorcerer's Stone in J.K. Rowling's first *Harry Potter* novel—to get it to fall asleep, you have to play the right music. When it comes to delivering feedback, the right music is an arrangement of three different notes: 1) giving timely feedback, 2) delivering formal and informal feedback and 3) framing feedback in language that signals psychological safety. Each one enhances trust in different and important ways. Together, they make the people on our team more receptive to our feedback and more likely to implement it. Whether you're coaching CrossFit Games athletes or leading a small business, this is the key. Execution is about forward progress toward a destination. Progress, by definition, implies struggle. **Execution is not measured by a lack of problems, but by how effectively your organization identifies and solves them.**

Give Timely Feedback

One of the reasons people are more receptive to coaching in a sports context than they are in a business setting has to do with expectations. Expectations powerfully influence how people experience reality. When we play sports, we understand intuitively that the coach is going to give us a lot of feedback. Because we're expecting it, we're not threatened or intimidated when we get it. To appreciate how this works, think about the last time you experienced turbulence on an airplane. If you're not expecting it, turbulence can be terrifying. The best pilots understand this and come on the intercom to let everyone know that they are expecting rough air. When the plane begins to shake five minutes later, you're ready for it. What might have been a terrifying experience ends up being only mildly uncomfortable, purely because the person in charge *told you what to expect.* At CFNE, I go out of my way to do this with all new employees. During the initial hiring process, I explain that feedback is the cornerstone of a culture that values growth and learning. I tell them that they should expect to receive feedback every day. **Understanding that feedback is a normal part of organizational life removes much of the anxiety and fear that often prevents people from acting on it.**

Traditionally, the vast majority of organizational feedback is given in the form of formal performance reviews that are conducted once or twice a year. You don't need to read the research to understand why this is a terrible way to get the most out of our people. If the essence of execution is closing the gaps in performance, it stands to reason that progress will be painfully slow if you only attempt to do it every six months. It would be like Bill Belichick skipping New England Patriots daily practices and only giving feedback to his players at formal performance reviews at the midpoint and at the end of the season—an absurd notion. Those formal biannual review sessions are important, but to improve results, coaches understand that they must be supplemented by continuous daily conversations with their players. As leaders, we should be doing the same—a Gallup study found that when leaders provided daily feedback (versus annual feedback), employees were *six times* more likely to implement it.[41] Accountability should look like coaching, *because it is coaching.*

Regular coaching conversations also shorten the feedback loop, which further enhances people's ability to act on new information. The shorter the time between a mistake and feedback, the greater the possibility for change. When people can remember the details of an event, they can more effectively determine how to use

---

41 Inc, Gallup. "Re-Engineering Performance Management." Gallup.Com. https://www.gallup.com/workplace/238064/re-engineering-performance-management.aspx

feedback to perform better in the future. It is very important to understand that the exact timing, however, depends on the type of skill that is being assessed. There are two types of skills: hard skills and soft skills. Hard skills are task-related and are usually black and white—either they were done or they weren't. Soft skills, on the other hand, are character-related—they are things like attitude, tonality and emotional intelligence.

Hard skills are easy to assess because they are objective. Did the coach hit all the points of performance for a squat? Was the procedure followed? Was the deadline met? Did the project come in under budget? The answer is usually simple yes or no. When it comes to hard skills, the most effective feedback is delivered in real time, as close to the example as possible.

Soft skills are the opposite. Because they are more subjective, soft skills require different timing. A coach demonstrating poor eye contact, one example of a soft skill, might mean that a coach isn't people smart—but it also might not. Maybe the coach was just having a bad day. The point is it's unclear. It's not a simple yes or no—you need more information. Soft-skill feedback should still be timely, but as leaders we should withhold feedback until a mistake can be identified as part of a consistent pattern. Without those additional data points, soft-skill feedback can feel like an unfair personal attack and do more harm than good. To be effective, our feedback has to feel valid and fair. That's what patterns allow us to do—objectify skills that are inherently subjective, which makes people more receptive to feedback.

Developing a coaching staff, as you might imagine, involves giving a lot of soft-skill feedback. A few years ago, one of my best coaches was a guy named Kevin. He was a phenomenal coach, a great guy, an amazing human being. Not long after he joined the CFNE coaching staff, I noticed a pattern in his body language. Kevin would make eye contact with the athlete he was working with, deliver effective coaching cues, and then ... abruptly drop his gaze. With his head down and eyes on the floor, Kevin would move down the line until he reached the next athlete. At that point, he would immediately pick his head back up, make eye contact and deliver his coaching cues. The problem was subtle—his head was down for just a few seconds at a time. Still, it was noticeable; it was an abrupt break in Kevin's otherwise strong and warm presence. The contrast was jarring. It made him briefly inaccessible to the athletes in his class. And it sometimes gave the impression that he didn't want to be there. Imagine how Kevin would have reacted if I had pulled him aside that morning. "Hey, Kev, I noticed that after you coached Meaghan's second lift, you dropped your head and broke eye contact with the room before you walked over to coach Tom." He'd probably feel how we'd all feel in that situation: *What the hell, man?* You're jumping down my throat because I dropped my gaze for a second, *one time?* It's weird. It's nitpicky. It's hard to take seriously. In that scenario, not only is Kevin not receptive to my feedback, he doubts the veracity of it—making him doubly unlikely to improve his performance. By waiting two weeks, I was able to observe Kevin's habit multiple times over the course of ten different classes and present my feedback as part of a pattern of examples. "Hey, Kevin, I've been watching you coach the past couple of weeks and I've noticed that you have a tendency to drop your head and break eye contact with the room when you're between athletes." This softer approach produces hard results. My feedback might still be hard for Kevin to hear, but as part of an observed pattern, he does not doubt that it's true. More importantly, the pattern tells him that my feedback isn't personal; waiting until I had multiple examples signals to his emotional brain that I gave him the benefit of the doubt. Not only is Kevin more likely to accept my soft-skill feedback and work on it, the trust I've earned in the process makes him more likely to accept and work on soft-skill feedback in the future.

Deliver Formal and Informal Feedback

Effective coaching requires more than just having frequent conversations with employees. To be effective, these conversations also have to feel comfortable. One of the things that makes formal performance reviews so uncomfortable is the fact that they tend to violate the aforementioned "give timely feedback" rule. If feedback is only given once or twice a year, it is almost by default a Big Scary Event. Team members are not used to getting feedback, so they interpret the criticism—no matter how constructive it may be—as a threat. To our human brains, everything about that scenario is cause for alarm. Which means even the best, most well-intentioned feedback delivered in this context will fall on deaf ears. This undermines the effectiveness of what could and should be a valuable opportunity to develop our teams.

The truth is effective leadership requires both formal and informal feedback. Again, it helps to think in terms of a football team. Yes, coaches deliver a lot of feedback on the practice field. But they also deliver a great deal of important feedback in more structured, formal environments, like film reviews and playbook meetings. It's no different in any other organization—to unlock the potential of our people and teams, we need to effectively deliver formal and informal feedback. The trick is not to completely dispense with traditional performance reviews. It's to make traditional performance reviews more comfortable by supplementing them with *informal* feedback. Just because it's not delivered in a meeting doesn't mean it can't be powerful; some of the most powerful and impactful coaching tends to happen in hallways, cubicles and other offhand moments.

At CFNE, informal feedback almost always happens right on the gym floor. Just before COVID-19, for example, a new coach named Alisha had begun coaching the 6:30 a.m. class I take each morning. She inherited the class from Elizabeth, who had coached it for the previous three years. As I did with Beth, I used class as an opportunity to develop Alisha's coaching. Every day, I noted one or two things she could improve, then took her aside after class to talk through them. We did this in the gym, next to one of the many whiteboards that line the walls or in a quiet corner out of earshot of members or other coaches. The informal setting helped put a new young coach at ease, which made her more receptive to feedback. Like Elizabeth before her, Alisha's performance improved rapidly. After six months—despite her relative inexperience—she was one of the best coaches CFNE had ever had. By the time she sat down for her first formal performance review, Alsiha had been receiving feedback informally almost every day for a year. As a result, our conversation during her annual review was remarkably comfortable, almost completely devoid of the usual anxiety, surprise and resentment that typically characterizes such meetings. By supplementing traditional forms of feedback with more informal ones, we increase the effectiveness of both. **As leaders, we can increase how effective our feedback is before we even open our mouths to speak.**

Signal Belonging

When we do start speaking, what we say and how we say it are incredibly important. Nothing has more of an impact on the effectiveness of feedback than the language we use to deliver it. To quote Albus Dumbledore: "Words are our most inexhaustible source of magic, capable of both inflicting injury and remedying it." The language we use to deliver feedback powerfully influences the emotional state of the people receiving it, which in turn dictates how effective it is.

A team of psychologists from Stanford, Yale and Columbia discovered that the exact words are less important than what those words signal to the brain. They found that the most effective feedback conveys something to the effect of: "I'm giving you this feedback because I have very high expectations and I know that you can reach them." This kind of constructive criticism boosted effort and performance so immensely that the research team nicknamed it "magical feedback." The magic, in this case, is a burst of belonging cues: *You are part of the group. This group is special; we have high standards here. I believe you can reach our high standards.* The psychological effect of these signals is so powerful, it's possible to predict the outcome of a conversational exchange by noting the presence or absence of them in the first moments of the interaction.[42]

---

42   Coyle, Daniel. The Culture Code: The Secrets of Highly Successful Groups. Bantam Books, 2018.

To understand how this works in practice, imagine you need to talk to one of your employees about a problem that's come up in their department. Which of the following conversation openers do you think will result in a productive meeting with an employee who is receptive to feedback?

Scenario A: "Hey, Morgan, do you have time to chat tomorrow around 3:00? Want to hear your thoughts on some improvements that could be made to take the facility up a notch."

Scenario B: "Morgan, please come to my office tomorrow at 3:00. We need to talk about why we're having problems with facility maintenance."

The core elements of the message are the same, but the language used creates two very different meanings. The tone of the first invitation signals to Morgan that he is safe and that his ideas are valued: *You are part of the group. This group is special. I believe you can reach our high standards.* The second invitation—which feels more like a legal summons to appear in court—could not be more opposite. The stiff language has all the sensitivity of a blunt axe. To Morgan, it's a signal that something is terribly wrong. For the next twenty-four hours, he is going to be consumed by the accusatory language of the last sentence—whatever the facility maintenance problems are, they are clearly being billed as his fault. With just twenty-one words, Morgan is knocked out of a flow state. He arrives at the meeting in the kind of defensive and indignant headspace that more often than not becomes a self-fulfilling prophecy.

It's worth pointing out that the point behind safe language is *results*. The second half of execution—indeed, this entire book—is about creating better results. We're not lacing our feedback with belonging cues for the sake of being polite. We're not focusing on word choice for the sake of being nice. If I didn't think belonging cues were so instrumental to unlocking potential, I wouldn't use them at all. **But they are, because nobody cares how much you know until they know how much you care.** Safe language is a system override that allows people to process information rationally instead of emotionally. This should not be confused with beating around the bush. To improve performance, feedback has to be crystal clear. If we do anything less than cut right to the chase, we waste everyone's time. The ability to be direct is the whole point—wrapping feedback in belonging cues allows us to be blunt without being threatening.

●

Execution occurs at the speed of trust. Whether you call it accountability or coaching, feedback that creates psychological safety is what allows us to create samepageness with the people we lead. Over time, that samepageness becomes trust, the portkey to a flow state. Trust is the magic that makes good coaching more effective. The more of it we earn, the more positive change we can create.

Whether you're coaching professional athletes or a team of twenty in a small business, trust is the most powerful competitive advantage you can have. When athletes trust their coach, their performance—and that of the entire team—can improve rapidly. The same is true beyond sports, in the organizations we lead. If we can learn how to deliver feedback in a way that builds trust, leaders can tap into the power of flow and unlock a similar level of performance among the people on our teams.

IF YOUR ACTIONS INSPIRE OTHERS TO DREAM MORE, LEARN MORE, DO MORE, AND BECOME MORE, YOU ARE A LEADER.

John Quincy Adams

EPILOGUE

LEAD

In the fall of 1974, an intensely introverted teenager named Larry enrolled at Indiana University. In his eighteen years of life, he had barely set foot outside his hometown of fewer than three thousand people. Now he suddenly found himself on a campus of more than thirty thousand undergraduates, and it unnerved him. His only chance of feeling at home in this foreign place, he knew, was the basketball team for which he had been heavily recruited. Prior to arriving at IU, Larry had been a high school basketball phenom. Everyone in Indiana knew the name on the back of his jersey: Bird.

If Larry Bird thought he might get some emotional support from his coaches, that notion was quickly dispelled. One night while walking down the street, Larry looked up and saw the Hoosiers head coach, Bob Knight, walking toward him. He stiffened and readied himself to speak to his head coach for the first time since arriving on campus. As Knight walked toward him, Larry said hello, but Knight blew by without saying a word. "Larry didn't say anything, but I could tell with his demeanor that his feelings were hurt," said a friend of Larry's who witnessed the interaction. "Larry was used to people being a lot nicer to him. He didn't like Coach Knight's personality." One month later, Larry Bird dropped out of the University of Indiana. His first impression of his coach proved accurate: Bob Knight had an abrasive personality and a violent temper that terrified the soft-spoken Bird. Under Knight, basketball did not feel like home. So he left, opting to finish his college career at Indiana State University. It says a lot that Larry Bird, the "Hick from French Lick" who elected to attend Indiana because of its proximity to his hometown, chose to leave the Hoosiers for a school that was both further away and had a far inferior basketball program.

The premature departure of Larry Bird had little apparent impact on Bob Knight's coaching career. Knight won 902 NCAA Division I men's college basketball games, a record at the time of his retirement. He is a Hall of Fame basketball coach. His abrasive coaching style didn't prevent him from achieving extraordinary results. Yet Larry Bird's decision to change programs suggests that he could have been even better. What would have happened if Knight had a coaching style more conducive to making teams trust each other, the organization and him as their leader? Knight, for his part, seemed to recognize this later in life. He regretted treating Bird so coldly. "Larry Bird is one of my great mistakes," he said. "I was negligent in realizing what Bird needed at that time in his life."

What would have happened if Larry Bird had stayed at Indiana and been developed by a Hall of Fame coach? Would the legendary Bird have been even better? Would Knight have achieved even more success? We'll never know, but it's safe to say that for all his achievements, Knight never succeeded in fully unlocking his own potential, or the potential of his athletes. That's what this book has been about, and the story of Bob Knight and Larry Bird underscores an important point: All of it is optional. You can ignore all the lessons in this book and still succeed by every metric used to measure success. **The risk of not leading with trust is not failure; it's failure to unlock your team's true, absolute potential. It's leaving potential on the table. It's "What if?"** This kind of risk is admittedly difficult to appreciate. How do you analyze the risk of not doing something? If you've made it this far, you appreciate it just fine. You're the kind of person who is haunted by "What if?" The idea that you didn't do all you could keeps you up at night. I wrote this book for you. Because most of us are not Bob Knight or Larry Bird or Katrin Davíðsdóttir … yet. Most of us are trying to break out of average and find greatness. No matter what kind of leader you are, this approach will help you do it.

I'm not going to lie: it's a hell of a journey. The trip will be a lot smoother for leaders who possess certain character traits:

---

10 ESSENTIAL LEADERSHIP CHARACTER TRAITS

1. **Passion:** Energy and enthusiasm for the vision
2. **Integrity:** Doing the right thing when no one is watching
3. **Presence:** Command the attention of a room with charisma
4. **Empathy:** Perceiving and understanding the emotions of others
5. **Positivity:** Optimism that the future will be better than the past
6. **Humility:** Understanding that the answers are outside ourselves
7. **Patience:** Calmly waiting in the face of frustration
8. **Curiosity:** Desire to build knowledge; open to new ideas
9. **Composure:** Unshakable in tense situations
10. **Self-Awareness:** Strong understanding of personal values and the ability to assess personal strengths and limitations

---

If you have all ten character traits in spades, you're ready to rock and roll. If you're missing a good chunk of them, it's going to be extremely difficult to implement the ideas in this book. As Jack Welch said, "Before you are a leader, success is all about growing yourself. When you become a leader, success is all about growing others." Character must precede leadership, because no one can pour from an empty cup.

Even with all the right character traits, leadership is extremely difficult. As Christine and I wrote this book, I was forced to confront an uncomfortable fact: I do not always follow my own advice. The wisdom I've developed as a leader over the years wages constant war against who I am as a person. I know how critical relationships are to my businesses, for example, but because I'm so introverted I tend to avoid the important and necessary work of developing them. I would much rather spend my time brainstorming, reading, researching, coaching and refining the vision of the business. I love the idea of disappearing into a hole to tinker away by myself, but it's not the best use of my time. That's where I am now: As CompTrain and CFNE continue to grow, my biggest challenge as a leader is to *consistently* implement the principles I've developed over the last decade. The activities on my calendar reflect how I have begun to prioritize things that will help me develop as a leader and unlock the potential of my team. Today, most of my "meetings" are not meetings at all, but large unstructured blocks of time dedicated to growing my relationships with the people I lead. As often as I can, I spend half or full days with the athletes I coach and the employees that work for me. No agenda, no specific goals—just talking and connecting and understanding. I still have to fight my introverted tendencies every day, but I've begun to win more battles than I lose.

It took me a decade and a half to figure out how to get the kind of results I expect for myself and my businesses, but gaining the knowledge was just the beginning. The real work is learning to consistently apply that knowledge within our organizations. **The principles in this book can only unlock the potential of the people and teams we lead if we are deeply and passionately engaged in implementing them every day.** If my experience is any indication, it's always going to feel hard. We're not ever going to feel like we're great at it. That's okay. Greatness, in my experience, is wherever someone is trying to find it.

Happy hunting.